THE HIDDEN CAVE

A Lucy Morgan Adventure Story

by

Gloria Barnett

SOFTWOOD BOOKS

SUFFOLK, UK

Published and Manufactured by Softwood Books
EU Responsible person: Maddy Glenn
Office 2, Wharfside House, Prentice Road, Stowmarket, Suffolk, IP14 1RD
www.softwoodbooks.com
hello@softwoodbooks.com

EU Rep:
Authorised Rep Compliance Ltd., Ground Floor, 71 Lower Baggot Street, Dublin, D02 P593, Ireland
www.arccompliance.com
info@arccompliance.com

Paperback ISBN: 9781838064341

Praise for

THE
HIDDEN CAVE

The Hidden Cave captivates young readers with the wonders of the sea in an enchanting blend of adventure and education.

Lucy is a daring young adventurer with a passion for diving. When a friend spots something mysterious hidden in the inky depths of the ocean their curiosity is aroused. Is it an underwater cave? Their discovery is thrilling, but Lucy, Jack and Solomon need to trust one another if they are to overcome the dangers ahead.

The Hidden Cave shines for its vivid storytelling and seamlessly integrates fascinating marine facts into the narrative, enhancing the realism of the tale. Lucy is courageous and her determination to help others make her an inspiring figure for young audiences.

'This is a story that not only captures the imagination but also encourages young readers to think critically about the marine world and their role in preserving it. '

(Literary Titan Review)

For Toby

Naopleon Wrasse

CHAPTER ONE
Strange Shape

'A year! It can't have been that long. It feels like only a few months.'

'IT WAS,' exclaimed Mum. '... exactly a year ago today we flew from London to start our new life here on Pontus.'

Mum looked across the breakfast table at me. 'Our lives have changed so much, especially for you, Lucy,' she said. 'You've got so involved with the sea creatures and learnt to swim and dive. You've made such good friends here, too.'

'It doesn't feel like a year's gone by,' I said, 'but I suppose it was last February, wasn't it?'

Mum nodded. 'We left on a cold, rainy day in London and arrived here in the Caribbean to the warmth of both the sun and the people.'

'I don't think I could choose between my favourite people here,' I said. 'Dan has helped me to understand the ocean and taught me to dive. Joel and Ellen help me to learn about the sea creatures and, of course, Jack and Sol are my real best friends.'

We packed away breakfast and went our separate ways. Mum off to work at the Community Library in St. Stephens town, just a short bus ride away, and me ... well, it was Saturday, so no school!

I walked across the road behind my house to the Dive Centre knowing that within half an hour, I'd be helping on Dan's dive boat.

Two hours later, I was three miles out to sea, happily wearing full dive kit and fifteen metres underwater.

Jack tapped me on the shoulder. Looking at me through his diving mask, he firstly pointed to his eyes, then indicated the coral reef below us.

His hands were silently communicating with me … 'look down there.'

I scanned the reef but couldn't work out what had his attention.

As I looked down, I could see the beautiful, colourful coral reef, full of strange and wonderful animals. There were hard corals, such as brain coral which had swirling, ridged patterns and staghorn coral, with sharp and spiky tips, attached to the reef in large structures. In amongst the hard corals, the sunlight from the surface shone through feathery soft corals and enhanced their exquisite colours. The different types of coral making up the structure of the reef was a home for a myriad of marine creatures, from tiny sea slugs to large fish and reptiles, like turtles.

I looked back at Jack, and he made a circle with his hands, then pointed downwards again.

What was he getting excited about? What had caught his attention on the coral reef below us? Was there an unusually large fish, or was there a tiny creature hiding inside one of the tall, purple pipe sponges? We'd often found small crabs and fish inside the tube-like bodies of the sponges, which stood silently amongst the corals, but I wasn't close enough to see inside the open-topped sponges which were at least ten metres below us.

I peered around, then noticed a strange dark area in the reef wall below us.

Was he was looking there?

I looked quizzically at him. I pointed to the roughly round shadowy section in the reef, made a circular shape with my hands and then pulled at the black material at the wrist of my wetsuit, trying to indicate the colour black.

Jack nodded excitedly. He then signed 'what?' with both his hands facing upwards and his shoulders pushed up into his neck.

I looked back and shook my head. I had no idea what the gloomy area was or exactly how wide it was. I estimated it was just on the limit of our depth range, at about twenty-five metres below the surface. I glanced at my depth gauge. We were now twenty metres down.

It was not easy to communicate anything more than basic signals underwater, so we'd have to discuss it when we got back on the boat.

We couldn't learn any more by looking at the strange shape from a distance and we certainly couldn't go down to investigate as we weren't just diving by ourselves.

On this dive, we were helping Dan and he'd asked Jack and I to do the 'tail-end Charlie' duty, diving at the back of his group of new dive students. The students were restricted to a depth of eighteen metres until they were more experienced and we had to stay nearby them.

I looked at the students ahead of us and those slightly above and decided we should be closer. I signalled to Jack to follow me so we could catch up with the others.

CHAPTER TWO
Diving with Students

Diving with Dan and his students on a Saturday morning was becoming a normal part of my life. I'd fallen in love with diving and I regularly found myself dreaming during a weekday school lesson, about what strange underwater creatures I'd find on my next dive. I often had to drag myself out of an imaginary dive when a teacher began talking to me.

Today's trip was part of a typical dive weekend. Dan had been teaching eight dive students all week, using the swimming pool to get them used to the dive equipment and learning all the safety rules, and today was their first adventure into the open water of the ocean.

We had the full Neptune Dive Centre 'team' of Dan, Sol, Jack and me, all onboard the dive boat. We'd helped Dan so often we could anticipate everything that was needed to be done, and skilfully avoided getting in each other's way in the restricted space of the boat.

I'd smiled when Dan had asked Jack and I to buddy up underwater and look after the students at the rear of the group. I was always pleased to help with this task, as I could swim slowly alongside the new divers, finding interesting creatures for them to look at as we progressed along the reef wall.

I can still remember my first dive in the sea. I know I was both scared and excited at the same time. When I first entered the water wearing diving kit, I was frightened of the unknown, yet as soon as I turned to look up, I could see a magical ceiling of sunlight coming through the surface above me. It was so beautiful, the sight helped to relax my nerves. I remember sinking quite fast until I pushed my control button to allow some air into my buoyancy jacket. Just a small amount of extra air enabled me to slow my descent and gave me a feeling of control in the alien environment.

When working with these students now, I knew how they were probably feeling. I could see nervousness in their eyes, so I kept close and encouraged them to add a little air into their jackets. Once they had stopped descending quite so quickly, they calmed down and began to get used to their surroundings.

By pointing out various sea creatures and communicating by hand signs, I could tell them what they were seeing, and this activity kept the students' minds busy and stopped them from worrying about their breathing. They could relax and start to enjoy their new environment.

We also had to ensure all the students kept up with the group and no one got lost.

Once everyone was safely underwater, Sol would take over as boat captain. He was just a year younger than Jack and me, and although he was a diver too, he was much better at driving the boat than I was. His job was to manoeuvre the boat slowly, following the bubbles from our air tanks at a short distance away and keeping the underwater propellers safely away from the divers. He would position the boat near the end of the reef where we'd planned to finish our dive, then switch off the engine and wait.

Sol was patiently watching as our dive finished and we all gradually surfaced. Our heads popped up out of the water close by and he helped everyone safely back on board the boat.

CHAPTER THREE

What is it?

'What were you pointing at, Jack?' I asked.

'That dark shadowy section of the reef,' he explained. 'I wasn't quite sure what it was ... but it was gloomy and mysterious-looking, sort of lurking in the reef wall.'

'Oh, right. Yes, I saw that. It looked like it was down at about twenty-five metres,' I said.

'Yep,' replied Jack, 'but what do you think it was?'

'At first I thought it might be a lump of old wreck that had crashed into the reef a long time ago,' I answered, 'but I don't think it was man-made. There didn't seem to be any boat-shaped metal or wooden bits sticking out anywhere. I don't think a wreck would look so round, either.'

'Dan!' I called. 'Did you see that murky, black area of the reef wall, down at about twenty-five metres?'

'No,' he said, shaking his head. 'Sorry ... I wasn't looking down much.' He came across to us and spoke more quietly so the students wouldn't hear him.

'I had to spend most of my time with those two students next to me at the front. They were getting themselves in a terrible tangle with their hoses and breathing apparatus.'

He paused to think.

'No. I've dived in this area a lot, but don't remember ever seeing anything like you've just described ... no, in fact I can't say I have ever seen anything unusual down there at all.'

Dan unzipped and tugged his wetsuit off. He pulled a pair of scruffy cropped-leg trousers over his wet swimming shorts and grabbed an old, torn tee shirt to wear. His long hair, styled in local plaits, was soaking wet and hung down dripping from his head. Covered in drying salt, he looked an absolute mess. Originally from Australia, Dan's white skin was very sun-tanned as he worked outside in the sun every day. As we travelled back to the jetty, he would gradually dry off in the warmth of the Caribbean sun, with the gentle wind blowing across the boat. I knew he'd probably stay dressed like this for the rest of the day. Dan was possibly the scruffiest person I'd ever met but I respected his ability to dive, and I was grateful he'd taught me to dive safely.

Dan took over the controls on the boat and we headed back to the Dive Centre jetty at Dolphin Beach.

Sol joined Jack and I as we tidied up the dive equipment at the back of the dive deck.

'The area looked like a dark circle,' said Jack, explaining our puzzle to Sol, 'although I think the bottom part of the shape, looked more like a line, but quite an uneven line.'

'All black ... dark and mysterious eh!' mused Sol. He shook his head. 'No, sorry, I've no idea.'

'Perhaps it was a new species of coral,' said Jack, 'Have you ever seen any black coral?'

'I don't think coral's very likely to be dark coloured,' I

said, 'it's always beautiful colours, like whites, yellows, pinks and pale purples. I know coral's actually an animal and not a plant, but it has algae living inside it, which makes oxygen from photosynthesis, like plants do, but if it was black it probably wouldn't be able to absorb the light it needs. No, I definitely don't think coral can be black … the same way plant leaves are never black either. It's all to do with needing the light for photosynthesis.'

'Crikey, Lucy,' said Jack, 'you sound like my science teacher.'

I just laughed. I loved to learn science facts and was always trying to think about how things worked.

Then my brain started to buzz.

'What if it wasn't some sort of animal or seaweed … what if it was a rock formation?'

I felt as if I was speaking my thoughts out loud.

Jack and Sol were looking puzzled.

'What if … yes! WHAT IF … IT WAS A CAVE!' I suggested, 'the black could be the lack of light coming out of the entrance hole. Yep, a cave, that could explain what we've seen.'

'Heck,' said Jack, 'a cave! You could be right, Lucy. I wonder how far back it goes inside the reef?'

'An underwater cave,' said Sol, 'Wow, that sounds exciting!'

'If it's no deeper than thirty metres, then we could dive

down to it,' I said. 'If we go inside and it doesn't go any deeper, then I think we'd be safe.'

'Do you think Dan would let us borrow the Rigid Inflatable Boat?' asked Jack, 'so we could go back and investigate it?'

'He'd probably lend us the RIB,' said Sol, 'but he'd expect one of us to stay and look after it. I didn't see any buoys around there for us to tie it up safely. If all three of us are going to dive to look at the cave, then we need to leave the boat somewhere safe.'

'The reef starts off in shallow water,' I said, 'quite close to that tiny beach area at the edge of the rainforest. If we left the RIB on that beach, we could swim out over the reef, and then dive down to take a look for the cave.'

'That sounds a brilliant idea, Lucy,' said Jack.

'Well, let's check with Joel later,' I said, 'he might have some ideas about it.'

CHAPTER FOUR

Cave

We found Joel, sitting at a picnic bench outside of Drifters restaurant. He had his afternoon cup of tea and was staring at a chess board.

'Hey, Grandad,' shouted Sol.

Joel put his hand up ... 'Shssh! I's thinking deep thoughts 'ere with this chess game.'

Sol quietly walked up behind Joel and looked over his shoulder.

'It's easy Grandad, look!' Sol leaned across and moved a knight. 'There you go ... checkmate!'

'How did you do that, young Sol?' Joel looked at him and started his rumbling laugh. 'You kids! Can't have you getting the better of me, can I? I'd better learn this game a bit quicker.' He looked around at the three of us standing waiting. 'So, what does you kids want now?'

Jack spurted out our puzzle.

'Well, now you's askin',' said Joel, looking thoughtful. 'Could it be a cave, eh?'

He stopped to scratch the beard stubble on his wrinkled old chin whilst he gave it some thought.

Joel was one of my favourite people. He always had time to answer any questions I had about the oceans, the coral reefs and the creatures who lived in them. After living in

London for so long, I felt I had so much to learn from him about my new home in the Caribbean.

Joel was also never afraid to admit he'd learnt something from others however old he was. He often admitted that some of his knowledge had come from Ellen.

When I first arrived on Pontus, Joel had explained. 'When Ellen came to live on Pontus Island a few years ago, she'd just retired from her scientific work in the USA. She bought that old house high up on Pirates' Peak. That's one of the highest areas of Pontus Island, that is.'

'Them local folks ...' Joel told us, 'they was a bit scared of Ellen at first. She seemed a bit strange with all her mumbling about big science words and living high up there all by herself with just those two dogs of hers, Charlie and Albert. But now folks have gotten used to her, just like we have.'

'I think she's great,' I said, 'her head's full of things I don't know about and I love going up to her house, sitting on the balcony with her, looking out to sea. She tells me all sorts of things, like the history of the pirates and this island. Up there I can imagine seeing pirate ships approaching, the way it had all happened centuries ago.'

'Yep, and Ellen ... well you know she can explain all about everyt'ing. Seems likes there's nothing that old woman, don't know.'

Joel and Ellen were often found head to head in Drifter's Bar where Ellen would answer Joel's questions about science things he'd not learnt at school. If Jack, Sol or I had any questions about the natural world though, Joel was as good as Ellen with his knowledge of oceans.

Between Joel and Ellen, all my questions about my new environment could be answered.

Joel began to explain the possibility of an underwater cave.

'Ellen, she's told me that most of these islands in the Caribbean Sea have popped up out of the water,' said Joel, 'and most of them were formed from underwater volcanoes, but that's not how this Pontus Island of ours was formed. Oh no! She's read that Pontus and some of the other islands on this side of the Caribbean have been formed from the coral reefs, pushed up from the seabed when the crust of the Earth jiggles around. She gave that some sort of fancy name … plate some'at or other?'

'Plate tectonics?' said Sol, 'I've been learning that at school.'

'Sounds like that might be the stuff,' said Joel.

'Anyhow, what about our cave?' asked Jack.

Joel was still looking thoughtful. 'An undersea cave … that'd be unusual that would,' he said, 'very unusual indeed. I reckons that cave'll go up through the reef. If you go inside that cave entrance, from way down there at twenty or so metres depth, then you'll probably be able to swim in the sea water and come upwards and you might come out where the reef surfaces and helps to form the island.'

'What? We could swim inside the cave and go up inside the reef? That sounds quite scary,' I said.

'I've often thought there could be a system of caves under Pirates' Peak,' said Joel. 'If they's there, then a cave structure like that'll be very old, but I don't remember anyone talking about finding an entrance to a cave from somewhere in the forest. Mind you, there's a lot of rainforest on that seaward side of the Peak and that's a story in itself. All 'em trees and such like. You could walk for days and not find the entrance to a cave. Anything could be in that forest. It's full of mysterious things. Strange plants and even stranger animals. But if you's be finding an underwater entrance, then you's might be able to find a whole cave system. I's not heard of anyone investigating any underwater caves yet on this island.'

I waited patiently, as he sat thinking and scratching his chin again.

'Mmm!' he said, almost whispering, 'you might be finding a cave system for the first time if you use an entrance coming from deep underwater. I reckons you's might be the first people to go into those caves ... yep, you's could be the first humans ever to go inside 'em.'

CHAPTER FIVE

Not Quite Telling the Truth

'We'll need to borrow Dan's RIB to get us back out to the reef,' I said.

'If we all want to dive, we'll need to find somewhere to safely tie up the RIB,' said Sol. 'We can't leave the boat bobbing about on the water, with no one on board. Trouble is I didn't see any buoys in Pirates' Peak Bay and it's far too deep for an anchor.'

'Well, we obviously all want to dive,' stated Jack, 'and if there's nothing to tie the RIB to, then we'll have to pull the RIB up onto the beach and perhaps hide it under the trees.'

'Still a bit worrying though,' I said, 'anyone could steal it.'

'We could put big leaves from the trees in the rainforest over it,' said Sol, 'camouflage it a bit.'

'Surely, leaving it for an hour or so should be okay,' said Jack.

'How do you think Dan will react if we tell him what we're planning to do?' asked Sol.

'His first thoughts will be to worry about whether we're planning to dive sensibly and safely,' I said.

'If we tell him about the possibility of an underwater cave, he'll probably stop us going by ourselves. I'm sure he'd want to come with us,' said Jack.

'Perhaps we should wait for him, then … go when he's not got any students to teach,' said Sol.

'Look,' said Jack firmly, 'if we promise each other to stop if anything looks dangerous, then we should be okay. I really want to investigate this, and it'd be great if we were the first people ever to go inside that cave.'

Jack leant forward, speaking more quietly, as if he was planning something secretively.

'Let's not tell Dan quite everything we plan to do. Just tell him we're diving on the reef.'

'Mmm. Alright,' I agreed reluctantly. 'but we'll need to make a good plan for what we need to take with us.'

'Apart from all our normal dive kit, I think we each need a big underwater torch,' Jack suggested.

'Dan's got some of those,' remembered Sol, 'he uses them for night diving with tourists sometimes. We'll be able to take three of those without him even noticing we've borrowed them.'

'Do you think we need some rope if we're going inside a cave?' asked Jack.

'If we're in the water, then we won't need to climb anywhere, will we?' said Sol.

'No, not while we're in the water,' said Jack, 'but Joel thought the cave might lead up under Pirates' Peak, so we might surface from the water, inside the cave.'

'This is all sounding a bit scary,' I said. 'Are we sure we want to do this by ourselves?'

'We can just go and have a look,' said Jack. 'If we find we do surface inside the cave, then we shouldn't investigate too far, but we might find a cave system that leads under the Peak. If we know there's definitely something to look for, we might be able to discover the way in later on, from the rainforest end on land.'

'Okay,' I said, 'but Jack, you'll have to ask Dan about borrowing the RIB. He's your uncle, and he seems to let you do most things. I don't think I can ask him. I'm not very good at lying.'

'I'm not going to lie,' Jack explained, 'it's more like just not quite telling him the whole truth.'

'I suppose if we dive on the reef, then find it is a cave and go inside to take a look, then surely Dan can't get too cross,' I said. 'We won't know for certain what's there till we dive, so we can't tell Dan in advance, can we? As long as we tell him about it later … I suppose that'll be okay, won't it?'

Sol and I exchanged a look. I certainly wasn't used to keeping information from Dan. It didn't feel quite right, but there was no way I was going to ask to borrow the RIB without telling him all our thoughts and it looked like Sol didn't want to do it either.

'Okay, Jack,' I said, 'you see if you can get the RIB for tomorrow.'

'If you can,' said Sol, 'then I'll borrow the torches when Dan's not in the equipment store.'

'I hope we're doing the right thing here,' I said, 'it sounds as if it could be a bit dangerous.'

'Nah!' said Jack, 'we'll be fine. Just like the raiders of the lost ark man, we'll be real explorers and be trying to find something never been seen before!'

CHAPTER SIX

Under Pirates' Peak

Jack didn't actually tell a lie, when he asked his Uncle Dan if he could borrow the RIB for Sunday, but he was able to keep his face straight and only told Dan about our plan to dive on the reef near Pirates' Peak.

'I thought about telling him our ideas, you know … that we think the dark shape could be a cave,' claimed Jack, 'but it sort of slipped my memory as I was talking to him.' He smiled with very big grin, his eyebrows wriggled and he placed his finger over his lips.

'Yes, okay, Jack,' I responded, 'but we must stop if there's anything dangerous and we'll tell him all about any new discovery when we get back. I'm not going to mention it to Mum, either.'

'I thought I'd just tell my parents we're diving on a reef,' said Sol. 'No problem.'

Sol pushed hard on the lever controlling the outboard motor. The speed was almost at maximum and from the bow to the centre, the rigid inflatable boat was lifting into the air and banging down hard on the surface of the sea in a rhythmic movement.

Sol had a look of gritted determination on his face as he kept control of the direction of the boat with his hands tightly gripping the outboard motor controls. It was a continuous battle as the waves had a natural desire to push against the boat, trying to turn us over, but Sol was in no mood to be beaten. He kept the speed up and the direction straight. His competence had grown over the summer with all the practice he'd had and I knew we were in safe hands.

Both Jack and I were trying to sit in the bow of the RIB as it was pitching upwards and then dropping back down. I was clinging onto the side handles and gasping for air as the exhilaration swept through my body. The wind, created by our fast movement across the water, was blowing my hair around my face and I could feel the throbbing of the big outboard engine through my feet. I tried to keep my face averted from the salty sea spray and turned to look behind us. As well as all the excitement for us in the boat, the sea seemed to get excited at our journey too. There was a stream of disturbed white water forming a straight wake behind the propellers as Sol kept the boat on course. Yet, only a few metres further behind us, the wake was already calming down and the sea was quickly returning to a peaceful, innocent flatness.

'It's not far to go now,' shouted Sol, 'we've passed the harbour entrance.'

We were heading for the tiny beach area below the rainforest on Pirates' Peak.

Another five minutes passed and Sol pulled back on the throttle. 'Here we are, folks. All part of the Sol Browne delivery service, door to door and no charge!' He smiled as he watched us both rub the salt spray off our faces.

'That was fun,' said Jack, 'thanks, Sol.'

'Get the rope ready, Jack, and I'll edge in under the trees,' said Sol. 'Over there looks like a good spot.' He was pointing ahead to the right.

'Lucy, keep an eye out for rocks underneath us as we get into the shallow water. I don't want to damage the propellers.'

I jumped into action. I leant over the bow looking down, and very quickly the seabed rose up to meet us as we moved closer to the sandy beach. There was no sign of sharp jagged rocks, just some boulders which had been smoothed by water movement over thousands of years.

Very close to the beach, and in shallow water, Jack took the rope and jumped off. Sol swivelled the large outboard motor round and pulled the propellers out of the water. The engine clicked into its resting mount on the stern of the boat.

Jack gently pulled on the rope, and the hard rubber boat obediently moved towards him, floating gently in the warm, blue, clear Caribbean Sea. As we got nearer to the beach, I slipped over the side of the boat, my toes splashing into the cool water. Sol quickly joined us. We all took a place near a side handle and pulled hard. Sol and I were on one side of the boat whilst Jack used his stronger muscles on the other side. Between us the boat gradually moved upwards across the sand and away from the surf line.

Jack made the boat fast with a rope, tying it around a tree trunk as Sol and I hunted for large leaves which had fallen from the trees above.

'Just a few big leaves will do,' said Jack. 'I don't expect there'll be anyone around here, but it'd be better to camouflage the boat a bit if we're going off and leaving it for a while.'

'Right, that's sorted then,' I said. I placed an extra-large, dark green leaf across the outboard engine. We left our small rucksacks with our lunch and water tucked up in the bow of the boat and covered them with enormous rainforest foliage.

I reached into the boat for the underwater torches and handed them out. We each checked the batteries were working.

'Okay, dive kit on then,' I said. 'I'll put my fins on in the water. It'll be easier to walk across the sand.'

We kitted up, walked back down the beach and into the sea.

CHAPTER SEVEN

Is it a Cave?

'Let's stay on the surface and just use our snorkels until we reach the far side of the reef,' I said, 'as that will save the air in our tanks for the dive.'

'Once we see the dark black circle from the surface, then we can dive down then, can't we?' said Jack. 'I can't wait to get down there.'

We snorkelled quickly across the surface, kicking our fins hard and following the line of the reef outwards.

Looking down through my mask, at the reef below me, I could see beautiful corals, and loads of my favourite fish, but we were on a mission. I was not stopping to admire the wildlife, I was kicking smoothly, making my way out to the western side of the reef where we'd seen the dark circle below.

We soon arrived over the area of the reef where Jack and I had first seen the dark black hole. I looked down. There it was.

Sol was seeing it for the first time. 'Yep, I agree,' he said, water dripping from his face as he pulled his head out of the water to talk. 'That could easily be a cave entrance. No way is it a wreck.'

'Okay then, are we ready?' I asked.

We all signed to each other to begin our dive. One by one we checked our air gauges, pulled a dump valve on our buoyancy jackets, breathed out and sank below the surface of the water.

It took only a couple of minutes to dive down to the black hole. Not only were we keen to investigate, we also wanted to get down quickly so as to not waste our air supply.

I ignored a variety of wildlife moving out of my way and concentrated on reaching the black shape beneath me.

It was definitely the entrance to a cave. Jack and I levelled out at the same time and swam closer to the reef. I checked my depth. Twenty-one metres ... a lot less than I'd anticipated. Good ...the less depth, the longer our air would last.

The water around the entrance was a clear turquoise colour, with sunlight shining through the surface from above creating a beautiful effect of sunrays stretching down from the surface.

I looked at the entrance. It felt very scary. The opening was totally black as if it was swallowing up the light coming towards it. I became very nervous and gazed at the entrance with trepidation. I'd never been in a cave on land, yet alone underwater. Would the cave swallow me up? What was I doing? Was this safe? What had I got myself into? Could I turn back now, and not go in?

I knew both Jack and Sol were keen to investigate so I pushed my questions to the back of my mind. The boys wouldn't want me to abandon the adventure of investigating what was obviously a cave. I felt I had no choice. I had to go on with the plan.

CHAPTER EIGHT
Going Up

When Sol caught up with us, we circled each other. I signed 'are you okay' to both of them and they replied they were. I checked my torch worked and indicated to the others to do the same. Then we switched them off again, saving the batteries until we were inside the cave itself.

The cave entrance was clearly defined as I looked at the jagged edges of reef leading to the darkness within. I looked towards the dark water ahead of us and switched on my torch. All of our torches shone ahead giving light to about four metres of distance ahead of us.

I signed to 'go forward' and pointed to the cave entrance.

Jack signed 'okay' and was nodding excitedly. Sol acknowledged the sign and we all set off together. The black hole was big enough for us all to enter, alongside each other but Jack kicked his fins hard and got ahead of Sol and myself.

I laughed to myself. Yes, Jack, you'll be the first one to go inside. You'll get your name in the history books!

Sol and I followed Jack inside.

Within a short distance, the cave tunnel we had entered began to turn upwards. It was getting dimmer too, as we swam away from our entrance hole. I checked my dive computer and watched as our depth decreased.

To begin with I felt a little nervous, perhaps because I knew if something went wrong, it wasn't going to be as easy as going straight up to the surface. If we suddenly had to abandon our dive, it would take us longer to get back to safety, as we would have to dive back down first, to exit the cave and then turn up towards the surface and fresh air.

I tried not to think about it but my mind insisted on telling me I was trapped. The cave walls felt as if they were closing in on me and it was soon pitch black all around me. The entrance seemed so far away. The light from the hole was so distant it looked like a star in a dark black sky. I tried to keep calm, breathe more slowly and control my use of air from my tank. Surely, I wasn't afraid of being in a confined space. I'd never had a problem before with going in a lift or anything, but for the first time in my life I felt a little anxious, perhaps because we were going inside a place we didn't know at all. Cave diving was completely unknown to us. I had to think carefully about our safety all the time. I stopped my worries from growing by constantly assessing our situation.

Air? Tick.

No problems? Tick.

I always felt it was my responsibility to ensure we were all safe. If something went wrong ... I'd have to make a quick decision about making our escape from the confinement of the tunnel.

I looked again at my dive computer. We were definitely going upwards.

Although Jack and Sol were probably excited about

entering the cave, I hoped they wouldn't forget the dangers of going up too quickly.

We had to be careful and ensure we went up slowly to allow the gases in our blood to adjust after the extra pressure of being deep underwater. We may even need to do a safety stop at five metres for three minutes. We all needed to remember to follow the rules of safe diving.

The light from my torch only shone a short distance into the blackness of the water. I was only just aware of the faint lights from Jack and Sol's torches. They were both slightly to my left but we were too far apart to see any dive signals between us. I was not able to communicate with them. We were not diving in buddy formation … we were not close together and not looking after each other.

They were too far away from me!

I felt as if I was alone in this strange environment, and it was a very scary feeling.

CHAPTER NINE
Dark Water

Although I had a torch, I seemed to need some sort of physical contact to calm me down. By being underwater, I was already in a state of weightlessness, which by itself, could be an unnerving situation, even though I was now an experienced diver.

However, in these conditions ... in almost complete darkness ... I was not able to see the boundary of the tunnel around me and there was no sunlight shining down from above to show me which way was up.

I felt very scared, so as I gently ascended through the warm, salty seawater, I reached my arm out to touch the side of the tunnel. It was comforting to feel the solidity of the rock alongside me. I allowed my fingers to run up the smooth surface, showing I was going upwards as I slowly kicked my fins. I was in control so I relaxed a little bit.

Then it began to feel freezing cold.

When we'd entered the sea at the beach the water temperature had been high. When we began our dive, deeper down to the strange black hole, it was still warm from the effect of the sun shining down from the surface ... but now, the temperature had fallen.

The sudden chill was accompanied by a changing visibility in front of my face. There was a strange cloudiness which was difficult to see through. The light from my torch looked out of focus in front of me. It was almost mystical. It reminded me of a science experiment we'd done in school when we'd mixed oil and water. The solution had turned to a strange murky, cloudy colour just like I was now seeing in front of my face. I blinked my eyes, but it made no difference, it was the water not my eyesight that was changing. Although I was completely safe, breathing from my own tank of air, and keeping my mask on ... the strange effect in front of my eyes and the freezing cold was playing games with my mind. I felt dizzy and shook my head.

I looked around for the others but could only see two indistinct shafts of light. That had to be Jack and Sol's torches. They looked so far away. I really didn't like what was happening. We shouldn't be separated so far apart, we should be together, as buddies, looking after each other. This was against all the rules of diving.

Then, my head popped out of the water. Had something propelled me upwards from below? No, calm down. Stop imagining things. I'd surfaced naturally from the force of kicking my fins.

I may have had my head out of what seemed like a lake, but it was still totally dark, apart from my torch. I adjusted the amount of air in my buoyancy jacket, so I could float with my head above the surface easily. Jack and Sol also appeared from the depths and I could see strips of light coming from their torches as they waved them around at the walls around us.

I took off my mask, so I could see more clearly. We were in an underground cave, and it smelt damp and musty. It was pitch black in parts of the cave where the torchlight couldn't reach. I felt chills rising up my spine and couldn't stop shivering. Was it the coldness of the water or was I scared of the unknown strangeness of our environment? We were inside a cave where possibly no person might have been before. The idea was doing extraordinary things to my mind. I kept questioning if I was trapped, then reminding myself of the way to exit the cave by diving back down to the entrance.

Was there air inside this cave? I squeezed my nostrils together to stop myself from breathing through my nose. My teeth clamped tightly onto my mouthpiece. I checked my air gauge. There was plenty of good clean air in my tank? But a big question needed answering. Was it safe to breathe the air in the cave? Could I take my mouthpiece out? I didn't have to wait long to find out.

I heard Jack's voice. He had removed his mouthpiece and I could see his head bobbing at the surface. He was only about ten metres away from me, but his voice was echoing around the large cavernous space around us. It sounded like Jack was talking to us from half a mile away with the echoes quietly repeating his words.

'It's okay, kay, kay … we can breathe the air in here, here, here' broadcast Jack and his echo. 'It's an enormous cave. We're surrounded by a strange rock formation, but I can feel cold air coming from somewhere and the air is fresh, so you can take your mouthpiece out and breathe.'

'Hey, that's clever, ever, ever …' Sol's voice had joined in with the echo, bouncing the sound around the cave as he breathed the air in the cave.

'The air feels a bit cold,' he said, 'but it seems okay.'

I decided that if I was to join in the conversation, then I'd have to breathe the air too. I gently took out my mouthpiece. My hands felt as if they were turning blue. I was becoming very cold, but I was able to breathe the air.

CHAPTER TEN
The Darkness

'It's freezing in here,' I said.

Jack had shone his torch around the cave walls when he suddenly yelled loudly.

My nerves made me jump and I shivered again.

'I think there's a tunnel, over there,' shouted Jack, waving his torch around. 'Can you see it? The tunnel leads off away from the cave. It looks like it's going upwards. That might be a way out of here. An exit.'

'The tunnel doesn't look very wide,' said Sol.

'We could probably clamber through the tunnel to see where it goes,' suggested Jack.

'It could be a bit dangerous,' I said. 'We've all got our dive kit. If we had to wriggle around rocks in a cave system, our dive tanks would be too heavy to carry.'

I could hear my own voice, I knew I was trying to give good advice, but was it all excuses?

I admitted to myself I was frightened. The only thing I wanted to do was to go back down the way we'd come, leave the cave system, get back into the blue water and surface to real air and sunlight.

I knew I couldn't admit to being scared to Jack and Sol, though. They seemed to be loving the whole adventure.

'Perhaps it leads to a cave system in the rainforest under Pirates' Peak,' said Sol.

'Yes,' said Jack, 'that's what Joel was telling us, wasn't it? In fact, I think I can see a faint light from the far end of the tunnel over on the left. I reckon there could be daylight coming through from above. Perhaps that's where the cave system starts beneath Pirates' Peak?'

'Well, even I'm not going to suggest we do the climbing from here,' said Jack. 'It looks far too slippery on those rocks.'

'I don't fancy breaking an ankle down here,' said Sol, 'I think we've discovered what we came for ... this is a cave and it has tunnels leading upwards to a possible entrance in the forest up there.'

'I don't think we can explore any more from here today,' I said. 'So, let's return the way we've come in and get ourselves back to the beach.'

I felt relieved the boys weren't insisting on investigating the cave further.

'Let's go back now,' said Sol. 'I'm freezing in this cold water.'

'The cold water is probably coming from the waterfalls above us on Pirates' Peak,' I said. I was forcing my mind to think clearly.

'I remember Joel saying water always finds its way downwards through the ground,' I said, 'constantly wearing down the rocks to form caves over thousands of years. I expect there's water running down into this tunnel system somewhere. That might explain why it suddenly got so cold in the water, just before we surfaced.'

'Yeah, sounds reasonable,' said Jack. 'But just before we go … let's all turn our torches off at the same time and see just how dark it really is.'

I was not happy about doing this. My torchlight had become very special to me. What if I couldn't turn the torch back on again?

CHAPTER ELEVEN
Scared of the Dark

I decided not to turn my torch off. Instead, I placed the torch tightly against the front of my buoyancy jacket and held it still. The light from the torch was trapped and it seemed as if I'd turned it off, but there was still a tiny glow of light escaping from around the edge of the torch. The comforting little circular glow stopped me from panicking.

Sol and Jack turned their torches off completely.

'Wow,' I could hear Jack's voice echoing around the cave. 'Isn't this great!' he shouted.

I heard my voice murmuring. 'No ... this is so scary ... it's the darkest of dark places I've ever been in.'

'I don't think I like this too much either, Lucy,' said Sol, and he switched his torch back on.

I sighed a big sigh of relief and drew my torch away from my body to release the light.

'Thank goodness,' I said. 'I'm never going to do that again. It was so creepy.'

'Really?' said Jack. '... I thought it was brilliant.'

'Right, then,' I said. 'Let's make a plan. We can go down again, back to the entrance. It'll be okay to go fast as we descend, but after we exit the cave, we'll have to remember the dive rules again, about going back up to the surface slowly again and doing a proper safety stop.'

'So, are we all ready?' I asked.

We signed 'go down' and accompanied by small splashes, we were soon all underwater again.

I was pleased to be leaving the cave. I'd not enjoyed either the complete darkness nor the feeling of being entirely enclosed so much. The water had been freezing and I couldn't be certain the air we'd breathed in the cave had been really fresh enough for what our bodies needed. I took deep breaths from the air in my tank. At least I knew the origin of the air I had in there and trusted I could breathe it safely.

I realised I was getting ahead of the others as I kicked my fins and quickly headed for the exit and the sea water surrounding the cave entrance. I could see the round circle of blue light at the end of the tunnel. To begin with the hole of light was small, but as I descended the hole got bigger and bigger. I was desperate to get out of the cave system and back to the environment I knew, of sea water, light and a surface I could see above me.

I exited the cave with a big sigh and turned, waiting for Jack and Sol to catch me up.

When they joined me, I signalled 'up' and we all headed back to the safety of the water surface, and real fresh air.

CHAPTER TWELVE
Pirates' Peak Reef

We surfaced from underwater and Jack and Sol both began talking at once. I felt so relieved to be back in the fresh air I could hardly talk at all. I concentrated on just breathing deeply.

Jack and Sol, though, couldn't stop chattering about our adventure of swimming into the cave. They were so excited.

'Look,' I said, 'I've still got plenty of air left in my tank. It's strange, it felt like we were in that tunnel and then in the cavern for so long ... yet it was only about thirty minutes in total. We've got enough air to go back down on to the shallow part of the reef and swim gently back to the beach underwater. It's always easier than trying to swim back along the surface, anyway. We might as well try to find some interesting marine animals now we're here.'

We planned to dive at just twelve metres below the surface, checked our air gauges and disappeared below the water again.

As we approached the reef an enormous fish came towards us. Was this fish dangerous, like the Titan triggerfish I'd met once before? I looked at it carefully. No, this was the opposite type to the trigger fish. This was a gentle giant, a huge Napoleon wrasse with a body larger than any of us. It saw us coming and moved towards us. It was obviously curious.

I gently kicked my fins and went slowly towards the enormous fish. It looked back at us with large eye movements, taking our images into his brain as visual data. It seemed to have no fear of us, whatsoever.

We stayed with the huge wrasse for a few minutes, admiring the incredibly intricate blue, green and yellow coloured patterns on its body. Then it decided to leave us. It went towards a large shoal of tiny glass fish. As it moved towards its next meal it opened its mouth. Its lips looked as if they were detaching from its mouth but they were sliding forwards creating what looked like a giant protruding straw as the lips extended outwards. The wrasse swam straight through the middle of the shoal. It sucked up little fish into its large straw-like mouth. It gulped as it swallowed its meal, then slowly the lips retracted, and the mouth closed, returning to its original shape. The fish turned and swam away from us. It had no need to fear us, nor should we be afraid of such a giant of the oceans. I was watching such a peaceful scene as it swam away.

Our peace was soon shattered however, as five barracudas appeared, quickly swimming towards the reef and coming straight for us. I recognised the stripes along the back of their bodies and although they were much smaller than the giant wrasse we'd just seen, I knew barracudas were dangerous. Their mouths were full of sharp, dagger-like teeth.

The fish got closer, so I indicated that Jack, Sol and I should stop in the water and stay very close together. We linked arms and stayed still. Did we look more like a big fish now? Would it put the barracudas off their attack?

The barracudas lost interest and moved away.

Phew, our pretending to be a big fish worked this time. Thank goodness for Joel, telling us so much about the sea creatures and how to behave to protect ourselves underwater. Joel had certainly helped us stay safe this time.

CHAPTER THIRTEEN
Beauty and Poison

The three of us went closer to the reef. It was full of tiny creatures. I pointed out a cute little Arrowhead crab nestling in some soft coral. It waved its arms about, trying to catch plankton floating through the water.

A sweetlips fish swam along the reef. Its yellow and black stripes showed up brightly amongst the hard corals. It stopped to scrape some algae off the coral then, munching as it swam, it carried on with its busy journey, paying no attention to us at all.

I saw a giant clam with its shell half-open drawing water into its body and filtering it for plankton. The clam was jammed between different coral structures in the reef, sitting immobile but with its two hinged shells open so it could feed. The inner part of the creature was brushed with a flamboyant purple colour, vibrant and sparkling in the sun which shone down through the water.

The clam had no eyes to see any approaching danger but must have felt the vibrations of my fins in the water and immediately shut its shell as I got closer.

Jack pointed at the coral. In amongst the fronds of the soft white corals was a white creature, so well camouflaged I could hardly distinguish it from the coral it was hiding in. It was a stone fish. Jack was giving us the signal for this creature by hitting his closed right-hand fist onto the top of his outstretched left hand.

He made sure we'd both seen his warning. This was a dangerous animal. It had poisonous spines. The stone fish didn't move much but lay in wait for a small fish to pass by, then would snap it up for its lunch.

The water was becoming shallower as the sea bed came up to greet us. We spent three minutes swimming around the top of the reef doing our five-metre safety stop, then surfaced.

We swam back to the beach and found the RIB. Swapping our dive equipment for the lunches we had packed up in the rucksacks, we found a comfortable spot to sit and eat.

'That was really good,' said Sol. 'The colours of some of those fish were so unusual. I think the giant Napoleon wrasse was my favourite. It was like a big friendly giant of the sea and the coloured patterns on its scales were awesome. But I didn't like the way those barracudas looked at us. I think they wanted a chunk of my hands for their meal. Scary!'

'Well done for spotting the stone fish too, Jack,' I said. 'I'm always amazed by how well they camouflage themselves.'

'Yeah, I only just spotted it in time to move away from it,' said Jack. 'Its camouflage nearly fooled me.'

'After we've finished eating,' I said, 'we can take a short walk in the forest behind us, just to get an idea of the conditions in there.'

We wandered through the trees close to the beach, and soon found it was becoming darker and much more humid. I started to sweat in the heat. Tall trees were stopping the light from entering above us. There were enormous plants, growing thickly, with long creeper like fronds completely stopping our progress.

'We need some big knives,' I said.

'What, like machetes?' asked Jack.

'Well, something sharp and big,' I suggested. 'It looks like we'll have to hack our way through all this dense foliage and trees before we'll see anything at all.'

'No wonder nobody's ever found an entrance to a cave around here,' said Sol. 'This is nearly impenetrable.'

'We'd better get a plan together,' I stated, 'and some decent equipment before we start exploring.'

'We'll need some anti-mosquito cream too,' said Jack, 'I'm getting bitten here. There are loads of insects flying around, and a lot of spider webs over there, too.'

'Hey,' I called out, 'there's an enormous insect on that leaf. I just got really close-up, and if you take a look at its mouth, its teeth are enormous. I wouldn't like a bite from that one.'

'I think I can hear something stepping on the dead leaves too,' said Jack. 'If you're quiet, you can hear the leaves crackling as something walks over them.'

'Something small though,' I said, 'perhaps a mouse?'

'Or a dragon!' teased Jack.

'Only a baby dragon,' I said, laughing, 'those dead leaves weren't being trampled by big feet. It sounded like a tiny animal, to me.'

'Let's go,' said Jack. 'I can't wait to come back and explore properly. We need to tell Joel what we've found today and he can help us plan our trip into the rainforest.'

'Mmm,' I said, 'I don't think he'll believe our story of hearing dragons, though, do you?'

CHAPTER FOURTEEN

Experience

Ellen came down to Drifters that evening.

Although she had sunglasses on and a big floppy hat to protect her against the heat of the sun, she could never be mistaken for a tourist. She always wore baggy trousers with loads of pockets, instead of the tourist uniform of shorts and tee-shirts. Instead of sandals, like most of us were wearing, she wore walking boots and she always wore a scarf … a long, green scarf that curled around her neck like a reptile.

'Aren't your feet hot in those boots, Ellen?' I asked as she arrived. She was puffing with the exertion of walking and slumped herself down at one of the picnic tables outside the restaurant.

'Boots?' she said absent-mindedly. 'Oh, yes, my boots. I like them because they're comfy and I don't get sand between my toes if I have to come walking along somewhere like this beach.'

Ellen was getting quite old, with wrinkly skin and dark brown spots splattered around her face. She had uncontrolled gingery hair, which I thought looked good, as it was colour co-ordinated with the freckle marks on her face. Although getting physically older, there was nothing wrong with Ellen's brain because despite how she looked, few people realised she had a long stream of letters after her name as she was Professor Ellen Roberts, Biologist, Geneticist and Mechanical Engineer! Her brain was as sharp as a razor.

Between Ellen and Joel, I was awash with information

about the island and its wildlife. There seemed to be nothing they didn't know about both.

I was keen to tell Ellen of our exploits inside the underwater cave. I quietly told her how I'd felt so isolated in the tunnel leading up to the cavern.

'I've felt like that,' she said quietly to me. 'I've only dived in sea caves a couple of times but both times, it really scared me. I've never been claustrophobic before but not being able to see the surface was a bit frightening for me.'

'It was cold too,' I said. 'I felt disorientated in the strange effect when the water got colder.'

'That'll be the thermocline,' said Ellen.

'The what?'

'It's when cold water's seeping in from a stream, or in this case probably from the waterfall rushing downhill from Pirates' Peak. That'd be very cold. Anyway, when that cold stuff meets the warm sea, the water visibility changes so it looks like you're staring through the wrinkled glass of a bathroom window. Was that what you saw?'

'Yes,' I said, 'that was it exactly. It was so strange. I couldn't see in front of me, even with the torch turned on. It was the spookiest feeling I've ever had.'

'But it didn't last long, did it?'

'Well, no. It wasn't long before I surfaced inside the cavern, but when I was ascending, the water still got colder and colder as I went upwards.'

Ellen was nodding, obviously remembering her own experiences. 'What's really strange,' she said, 'is that the thermocline you experienced is exactly the opposite effect to swimming in the open sea. In the sea, the sun warms the surface, but cold water can come up from the dark depths underneath you, into which the sun doesn't shine. Sometimes you get a cold spot, coming in sideways at you from a river, or a stream on land. You can be kicking your fins, minding your own business, then wham! Intense cold hits you from a stream coming from just below the land, and into the sea. You get an eerie feeling with that too, and you'll get the same glassy effect in the water when the two temperatures meet up. It's all strange stuff, and very creepy. But going upwards into a cave, you were getting the cold water coming downwards from above you.'

CHAPTER FIFTEEN
Telling the Tale

Jack and Sol had gone to find Joel and I saw all three of them approaching.

'Hi Joel,' said Ellen, 'these three have been having a great time.'

'Yep, look at you kids, all jumping up and down with excitement. I guess, you found a cave. Did it have tunnels that lead up under Pirates' Peak, then?' he asked.

We were all nodding. 'Yeah,' said Jack, 'we found the cave entrance and like you said, Joel, the tunnel went upwards.'

'We swam up until we surfaced inside the cavern,' said Sol. 'It was like being in a lake inside the cave.'

'There was a tunnel leading out,' Jack explained, 'but the rocks were too slippery for us to get out of the water and look around, and we couldn't climb around in our dive gear easily.'

'So, we stayed in the lake,' said Sol, 'but I was sure I could see a pinprick of daylight in the distance, as I looked up through a tunnel. We could certainly feel cold air coming down too.'

'I reckon the tunnel meandered upwards,' said Jack. 'It might be difficult to clamber over the rocks and scramble around the big ones ... but if we'd investigated, I reckon the cave would've come out on land again.'

'I agree,' I interrupted, joining in with the excitement,

'the tunnel was leading upwards towards Pirates' Peak. I'd been keeping an eye on my compass. The cave should come out in the rainforest somewhere.'

'Sounds to me like you needs to go investigate all that system on land next,' said Joel.

We'd all been so excited that we hadn't heard Dan come up behind us.

'What's all this about then? What have you been up to?' he asked.

The three of us looked at each other. We hadn't told Dan about our plan to go into the cave.

'Well, we came across that black hole again, Dan,' said Jack. 'So, as we were down there, we thought we'd have a look at it. It's a cave entrance and we found it went upwards, and probably leads back to the rainforest on Pirates' Peak.'

'What you went diving inside a cave?' Dan looked anxious. 'I've not taught you all the special techniques you need for that.' As he frowned his eyebrows nearly joined together. 'I thought I'd taught you three to keep safe?'

'No, we were alright, Uncle Dan,' said Jack, 'we stayed as a buddy team all the time and were very careful.'

I glanced across at Jack. That wasn't quite as I remembered it.

'Mmmm!' Dan seemed to be thinking about our adventure and he asked a few more questions but luckily, he didn't get cross with us.

'I guess I'd have wanted to go and have a look myself, if I'd been there,' he said.

'It's okay, Dan,' said Jack, 'we were being very safe.'

'Well, at least you're all here, unharmed. I don't want your Mum getting worried about you though, Lucy.' Dan looked directly at me. 'Just promise me, that you'll always dive carefully, all three of you.'

'No problem, Dan,' I said innocently, 'we always dive sensibly.'

We may not have had any clue what to expect or what we would find as we entered the cave, but I'd always been thinking about keeping safe. So, I wasn't really telling Dan a lie.

Was I?

CHAPTER SIXTEEN

The History of Pirates' Peak

Sol moved across to sit next to Ellen.

'Your house is up on Pirates' Peak, isn't it, Ellen?' he asked. 'How did Pirates' Peak get its name?'

Ellen was quick to answer and was smiling. 'That's easy, you can see how it got its name if you come and sit in my garden. Lucy came up a while ago, and we sat on the balcony. The peak is so high you can see for miles in all directions. In the olden days, if the islanders looked out from there, they could see the pirate ships coming and had time to think of ways to frighten them away.'

'Crikey,' said Jack. 'Are you talking about real pirates?'

'Yes,' said Ellen. 'One story I heard was the islanders got some old wooden boats and put them at the entrance to Jude's Bay harbour. The islanders could watch from up on Pirates' Peak and raise a flag if a pirate ship was coming towards the island. The flag was a signal to the men at the harbour, who would then set fire to the old boats. They had to be careful not to burn any newer fishermen's boats whilst they were trying to frighten away the pirates, but it was mostly a good idea and the pirate ship would turn away from entering the harbour because of the thick smoke and flames. The pirates' boats were also made of wood, so the pirates didn't want their ships to come into a dangerous fire zone. It was quite clever really.'

'Wow! That sounds a brilliant plan,' said Jack.

'You can see for miles. It's one of the main reasons I bought the house,' said Ellen.

'It's beautiful up at your house, Ellen,' I said, 'I loved it when I came up with Dan all those months ago. I love your two dogs too!'

'Next time you come up I'll show you some old pirates' documents. I found them when I moved into the house. I should take them down to the Pontus Library really, but I wanted to read them properly first, and I've not had time. I remember there's a map there too.'

'A map,' yelled Jack, 'it might show where there's some treasure been stashed.'

'Well, I'll have to find the papers first, I know I put them somewhere safe in the house. Then we'll read all about it sometime,' said Ellen.

'What do you know about the pirates that used to come to this island?' Jack asked Ellen.

'Well, the history books are a lot kinder to those pirates than the myths and legends are,' she said. 'All the myths and legends have pirates as being bloodthirsty killers, but some of them were privateers. A bit like trading ships going from one island to another.'

'Yes, seizing an opportunity they called it,' said Joel, 'I don't think they's as innocent as Ellen makes 'em out to be, though. They'd see some'at and want it. Taking things from the islanders and probably hurting them when 'em stole it all. Then they'd sell their booty to people of either another island, or even sail back to Europe, to Portugal or Spain and sell stuff there.'

'What sort of stuff did they steal from the locals?' I asked.

'Oh well, silver was popular,' said Joel, slipping into his telling-a-tale style of leaning forward and talking more quietly. 'Silver was mined for centuries before 'em pirates and privateers came along and stole it all. I heard there be museums in Spain with lots of Caribbean silver on display. Now, yous has to ask yerselves, how did they get all that, eh?'

Joel leaned in further and we were all quietly waiting for the next nugget of information.

'Yous still gets tales of pirates, and tunnels and old treasure on this island, but nobody's found any such things.'

'Well, perhaps it's time we changed all that,' said Jack. 'I think we need to try to find the cave system we saw from underwater.'

'We certainly need to do that,' I said loudly, as a tingle of excitement rushed through my body, all the way from my stomach to my mouth. 'I think we've got some investigating to do, don't you?'

I was looking at Jack and Sol as I spoke. They were both nodding furiously.

I couldn't wait to start our search.

CHAPTER SEVENTEEN
Machetes

'The forest is very thick, Joel,' I said, 'it'll take us ages to cut a way through some of the tree branches and big plants.'

'I reckons there some of them big machete knives at the back o' my shed. If yous finds 'em then just you be sure not to cut yerselfs on them sharp blades. But they should get you cutting through 'em bushes alright.'

We searched Joel's shed for the large knives. It was a mass of higgledy-piggledy stuff. He obviously left everything that he found in there, hoping perhaps one day there'd be a use for all of it.

The knives seemed a bit rusty, so Jack got a cloth and a drop of engine oil from his Dad's garage and cleaned them up.

He kept the knives well out of sight of his Mum as he worked on them. 'No point in getting Mum worried,' he said, as he returned with shiny sharp blades on the knives.'

'No way,' I said, 'I'm not telling my Mum everything we're planning to do, either. I know we'll be careful, but she'd just be sitting and worrying. I don't want to do that to her.'

Dan had agreed to us borrowing the RIB on the following Sunday when we were next free from either having to go to school or help on the Dive Centre boat.

'We need to do a risk assessment,' I said. 'I've learnt about that in science at school.'

I also made a list of what we needed. We all called things out as we thought of something new.

'Right,' I said, busily writing the list. 'That's rucksacks, machetes, torches, compass, some rope and we'll all need an old tee-shirt to wrap the machetes safely before we put them in the rucksacks. Anything else?'

'Well, food!' said Jack. 'I'll need food, if we're cutting down half a rainforest.'

'Better not be half a rainforest, Jack,' I said. 'We'd be in trouble for destroying the natural environment.'

Jack offered to carry the rope, so his rucksack was heavier than mine, or Sol's.

'I'll put in a small first aid kit, as an extra,' I said, 'and insect repellent too.'

'Okay,' said Sol, 'I'll put in some spare torch batteries too.'

'Have we all got water bottles?' I asked. The two boys nodded. We were ready.

When Sunday dawned, there was hardly any breeze. There had been a rain shower in the night, but it was already hot, even though it was still early in the morning.

The three of us met at the jetty. Putting our rucksacks safely into the RIB, we zoomed across the calm, flat water. When we passed Pontus Harbour, it was strangely quiet because of the early hour. There was an atmosphere of a lazy Sunday morning about the harbour, with no noise at all coming from the boat repair sheds. Fishing boats were still, hardly shifting on their anchor chains. The daytime tourist trade hadn't yet started so there were no ringing voices of tourist workers calling out to offer boat trips. There were no boats going in or out of the harbour to see us make our way to our secret beach.

We arrived at the same sandy area under Pirates' Peak, where we'd been before. We unloaded our rucksacks and camouflaged the RIB as much as we could under the trees at the back of the sand. Then we entered the rainforest.

There was no breeze in the rainforest at all. It was hot, sticky and humid. I looked around but could only see an impenetrable wall of green. The air seemed heavy in my nose as I tried to breathe. My eyes had to adjust to the shadowy light, and I could hear the noises of the animals again. Dead leaves being disturbed, invisible birds calling in the branches, unseen as the foliage was so thick. Even my mouth was a source of sensations. I tried to keep my mouth closed so insects wouldn't fly inside, but I had to help my breathing by opening my mouth and taking deep breaths. I could feel dust in the air catching on my tongue and smells of the foliage hung in the air, reminding me of different types of herbs.

As we started work on hacking a pathway through the forest, my clothes began to stick to my body, and sweat poured from my forehead.

To begin with our task of cutting back the plants and trees branches took us ages. We gradually chopped back the foliage and made a pathway for ourselves through the forest. Then ... we made a discovery! We came upon an existing path. We checked with the compass and found that the path led in two directions. We turned right and walked downwards to see where the path had come from. It went down to the beach, with the entrance to the path tucked away at the opposite end to where we had left our RIB. The entrance to the path was not obvious, it was well hidden among the trees.

'I think if we come back this way, it would be quite easy to walk along the edge of the forest and back to our boat,' I suggested, 'and the compass is telling me the path is leading up into the rainforest, where we want to go. So, let's not bother cutting another path, let's just use this one.'

'Looks like someone else has definitely been here,' said Jack. He was standing on the beach and looking at the trees. 'If you look at the marks in the sand, I think someone has pulled up a boat just like we've done. Pulled it up away from the sea and tucked it in the foliage under the trees.'

'Well, there's no boat here now,' I said. 'Just us. I wonder who else knows about this area of beach?'

CHAPTER EIGHTEEN
A Well-Trodden Path

'No point in standing looking at the sea here,' said Jack, 'let's go back up and start to search for our cave system.'

'I wonder if whoever has been here before us has already found a cave,' I said, 'this path looks as if it's used quite regularly.'

We walked up the path, passing where our machetes had created our own route through the forest from the other end.

'Looks like someone's used some sort of trolley along here,' said Sol, 'it looks to me like wheels have made marks in the sand. There's been lots of feet treading on this sand, too.'

'The pathway is quite hard underfoot here,' I said, 'so to make a mark through this sand the trolley must've been quite heavy,' I said.

'Hey, Lucy,' said Jack, 'you and Sol make good detectives.'

'Whoa! Stop!' I called out, 'look at this.' Jack and Sol came crowding around me as I stood still and looked down at my feet.

'Have you noticed this pathway is moving?' I said. 'My feet have disappeared. Ouch, that tickles!'

It's a long line of ants!' said Sol.

'They're leaf-cutter ants,' I said. 'I've seen them on television. Look they're marching across the path.'

'Yeah, they're coming on a route from deep in the forest,' said Jack, 'then crossing the path and heading over the other side.'

'Just look at them. They're tiny and each one of them is carrying a bit of a leaf,' said Sol.

'Yes, I've heard of these creatures,' I said. 'Each bit of leaf they are carrying actually weighs more than their own body. They bite off a bit of leaf, which if you look very closely, is why the leaves are all edged with small teeth marks. Then they carry their tiny bit of leaf back to their nest. I suppose they use the leaves for food or nesting materials.'

'That's really amazing,' said Jack, 'they must be so strong to carry something weighing more than themselves. Wow! I could watch these little creatures for ever. There must be thousands of them. Look there's more, coming along behind.'

I stood up and looked around. We were only a few paces away from the rainforest and I gazed through the trees.

'There are some strange looking spiders in amongst those trees, too,' I said. 'I wasn't watching out for anything like that earlier, I was too busy wielding my big machete. But now I've stopped to look, it's incredible. Look, big spiderwebs and the most beautiful butterflies.'

We were all quiet just looking at the insect life, then I heard bird noise above me. Something was calling, then another bird whistled. My ears were tuning in to the sounds of the forest. What was that? This time I could hear the sound of a larger creature walking on the dead leaves beneath the trees. A loud crackling, snapping sound.

'That's not a baby dragon,' said Jack. 'Do they have tigers in this forest?'

'No, Jack,' I laughed. 'I don't think so, but there must be some ground dwelling creatures in here. People say that rats are always close by, wherever you are. But I think there might be strange mammals that live in a rainforest like this, and that one certainly sounded a bit bigger than we've heard before.'

'Anyhow, we came to find a cave,' said Jack. 'Let's get on.'

'I'm just wondering who's been through here,' I said. 'Someone's cut through this area of forest and has been using this path. I don't think the entrance from the sea and beach end would be very visible to anyone sailing past. I can't think why the path is so well hidden.'

'I think I can guess,' said Jack, 'I reckon this … is a pirates' path.'

CHAPTER NINETEEN
Smugglers?

'Oh, come on, Jack ... pirates haven't been around these islands for a couple of hundred years or more. This path has been used recently. You can see the way the plants at the sides of the path have been broken as something has pushed past them. That's happened recently, it can't be pirates now.'

'No,' said Sol, 'but it could be smugglers. My uncle Sam was telling me about the smugglers who steal precious artefacts from some of the old Mayan city ruins in Mexico. It seems it's a big trade. Like the old pirates who used to steal people's silver and then take it to Europe. This island could be a stopping off point from Mexico around to the east side of the USA. Uncle Sam thought he had some very secretive people in his taxi in St. Stephens a few weeks ago. People in the back of his taxi usually talk to him but not these ones. He thought they were talking about gold. Perhaps they were smugglers.'

'I think Sol could be right,' said Jack, 'These people are really just thieves, but if they can find the right people who'll pay them for what they've stolen I've heard they earn lots of money. If they're caught of course, they go to gaol for a very long time.'

'Whoever cut back all the bushes and trees to make this pathway must've wanted to do it for a good reason,' said Sol, 'and it sounds like it could be smugglers of ancient art and stuff.'

'I'm happy they've done all the hard work for us cutting a path through the forest,' I said. 'I don't really think the three of us would've been able to get much further using our old machetes. But we have a clear path now. What we don't know is where this path leads?'

'There's only one way to find out,' said Jack, 'and I don't think anyone is here at the moment as there's no boat on the beach.'

'Okay, let's go,' said Sol, 'let's hope the path leads to a cave system.'

As we walked along the path, I noticed some really large boulders. I looked up at the rocky cliff above me. These enormous rocks must have come crashing down from Pirates' Peak. I remembered our flight in the light aircraft a few months ago, when we'd flown around the mountain and over Ellen's house. We had seen the small beach, the rainforest and also an enormous waterfall. There was a large area of the forest about halfway down from Ellen's house where all the trees had been flattened and bare white limestone rock was showing through. Ellen had suggested the big rocks had been undermined by the waterfall, had come loose and fallen away from the cliff face exposing the white surface beneath. I remember looking down from the window of the plane and seeing large rocks near the bottom of the forest.

I looked up at the Peak and realised we were standing beneath the very area we'd seen from the aircraft. We had stood on the beach and now we were in the part of the forest where the boulders had fallen. I could see large boulders around us as we walked along the path.

I looked more carefully at the rocks. They were not just large … they were enormous and there was no way any of us could push or move them.

I hoped there was going to be a cave system ahead, but I hoped even more that the boulders were not going to stop us from entering them.

'How much further?' asked Sol, 'this is hard work.'

We were still walking steadily up the hilly path and around the boulders.

'No, idea,' I said. 'We don't even know if we're heading towards a cave yet.'

'You never know,' said Jack, 'if we do find a cave, perhaps it'll have been used by gold smuggling pirates in the past. We might even find some pirate treasure.'

CHAPTER TWENTY
Looking for a Cave

The rainforest completely covered the mountains in the south-east region of Pontus Island. We had walked through from the bottom of the dense forest following the small path. Although the path had obviously been used in the past, I wasn't sure how long it might have been since anyone had climbed up the mountain using this route.

Jack, Sol and I had become fascinated by the idea of an finding an unknown cave and I was so excited I stopped talking. I saved every lungful of air to help me walk up the inclined path.

The path twisted and turned as it negotiated the sharp rise in height. I looked around me and behind me. I estimated we'd come up the side of the mountain for nearly a kilometre. I was able to look down at the sea behind us. Still no one in sight. Was that a boat approaching? There was certainly something on the horizon, but it needed to be closer before I could decide if it was friend or foe.

I turned back to the task of pushing myself up the mountain side. It had become steeper as we moved upwards. Then the path flattened out.

The outlook ahead was changing. The trees were less dense. I realised the path had taken us to an exposed section of the rock which made up the mountain.

The path had definitely guided us where to come. I could clearly see the big rock wall above me, exposed from its protective tree covering. I looked ahead of me. What was between the trees, over by the rocky cliff wall? It seemed like a dark shadow.

'It looks like a cave entrance over here,' said Jack, as he moved closer. 'Yeah, I can see it now.'

I walked on. Now I could glimpse something slightly different in the cliff face. Yes! There was a small cave entrance hidden amongst the rainforest foliage.

I thought the sun had darkened but realised as we walked closer to the cave entrance that plants were climbing over our heads and we were in a damp, clammy, humid environment.

'Gosh, it's very gloomy,' I said. 'I don't think the sun ever shines through the thick trees into this area of forest.'

Sol and I quickly caught up as Jack began to climb over the rocks outside the entrance.

'Careful, Jack,' said Sol. 'Is it slippery?'

'No, it's not been too bad so far but be careful you two, it's now getting a bit slimy where the plants have covered the rocks. They might've got wet in that early rain shower this morning.'

'Or the water might've come down from the waterfall above us,' I suggested.

'Well,' panted Jack breathlessly. 'However, the wetness got here, I can definitely say the surface is really slippery now. You'll have to go really slowly, here.'

Jack had clambered over the slimy boulders and had bent down to creep through the narrow entrance. The cave was so dark I could hardly see him. He called out. We heard his voice echo back at him.

'Hey, did you hear that? That's a cool echo,' shouted Jack.

'It's just as well no one else seems to be around,' I said to Sol, 'Jack's making a lot of noise.'

'Hey, Jack, be a bit quieter!' called Sol. 'You never know, there might be someone still inside there.'

There was no answer from Jack. He'd disappeared into the cave.

Sol and I carefully climbed our way over the boulders. The cave entrance was quite small and I had to bend my head to get inside. Sol and I moved inside the cave to where Jack was standing.

I was soon reminded that I'd left the sun outside. Despite only having gone a metre inside from the cave entrance, I began to feel very cold. I looked up. The cave roof was quite high behind the entrance but reduced in height the further I looked across the cave. There seemed to be a tunnel further in, looking dark, scary and mysterious. I stared at the walls of the cave. It was made of limestone and I could just see different layers, one on top of another, with bands of shells and hard materials between the layers. The layers weren't evenly patterned though and there were large areas where there were no exposed shells at all. I wanted to look more closely with my torch to see if I could find some fossils in the limestone but knew I would have to wait for an opportunity later. At least I had identified the basic cave structure.

Then something flapped around my face!

CHAPTER TWENTY-ONE
Nasty Smell

'Oh,' I screamed, 'go away!' I threw my hands up to protect myself.

My nerves were on edge, but it was a harmless creature. A large, beautiful, iridescent butterfly continued to flap around my face as I walked further inside. I shook my head to stop it landing on me.

'Do you think there are any animals in here?' I whispered, almost speaking to myself. There was a musty smell of wet foliage inside the cave, plus a different, more pungent and nasty smell I couldn't recognise.

I think we've got bats in the roof of the cave,' said Jack. 'There's lots of white stuff on the floor underneath them.'

'I think that's their poo,' said Sol. 'I've read about that in books and I know we definitely have bats on the island.'

'That might be the cause of the nasty smell I don't recognise,' I said. 'Charming! Bat poo! Not the sort of treasure I expected to find.'

'Are bats dangerous?' asked Jack.

'No,' said Sol, 'I think the bats we have on Pontus are fairly harmless.'

'I wonder if we'll see them,' said Jack, 'I can remember a film once when someone was attacked by bats and they were flying all around their heads.'

'I think bats come out at night?' I said. 'Don't they, Sol?'

Sol nodded. 'Yeah, I think we're safe from bats.'

'Aarghh!' yelled Jack, 'what was that? I thought you said bats only fly at night. I've just been dive-bombed by a flying bat.'

'No, Jack,' I said, 'I saw it fly in. It's only a swallow. I watched where it went and it obviously has a nest just inside the roof of the cave, really close to the entrance above your head.'

'A swallow! What, a little bird?' said Jack.

'Yes, Jack,' I said, 'I think you're quite safe.'

'Jack ... if you could be frightened by a swallow,' said Sol, 'then what are you going to do if we find smugglers or pirates in here?'

Jack ignored him.

'Do you reckon the cave is old enough to be an old haunt from when there were pirates in the Caribbean?' Jack asked.

'I think so,' I answered, 'I think caves and rock formations take hundreds of years to form and change, and we've no idea what the cave might have been used for in the past.'

'Stashing all the pirates' treasure hauls,' said Jack. 'I bet we'll find some treasure in here.'

'What!' said Sol, 'I can't believe you, Jack ... d'you honestly think the pirates might have forgotten about some hidden treasure? Having fought and pirated other big galleons to get their precious booty, you think they'll have just chucked it in a corner of the cave and gone off and left it?'

'Well, when you put it like that, I suppose it's not very likely,' said Jack, 'but it'll be great to search the cave, won't it?'

'Okay, it's what we've come for,' I said. 'Let's get our torches out and start searching.'

We all stopped and rummaged in our rucksacks.

'I should have put brought a cutlass or a sword or something with me to fight off the 'Skeletons of Pirates' Past,' I joked. 'I hope they won't mind us disturbing them after all these hundreds of years. 'Okay, you both ready?' I asked.

Jack and Sol nodded, then strode off ahead of me.

Jack was desperate to be in the lead. 'I reckon this cave will hold lots of secrets,' he said hopefully.

'Could do,' I said, 'let's just hope it doesn't contain anything too scary.'

CHAPTER TWENTY-TWO

Inside the Cave

Sol and I followed Jack deeper into the cave.

'Whoa,' yelled Sol, as he took a tumble.

'Are you okay, Sol?' I asked.

'Yep, I just slipped on the rocks here. Be careful everyone, there's lots of that green soggy slime inside the cave here at the back.'

'It's probably due to the damp sea air blowing in through the entrance,' I said.

I swung my torch around.

The cave floor looked wet with the odd puddle reflecting the light of my torch. There were lots of loose boulders piled up, lodged all around us.

I picked my way across the large stones, carefully placing each foot to avoid the slimy dampness.

'You can really imagine smugglers or pirates in here, can't you?' I said.

'Actually,' announced Jack, 'I think I might have found something.'

I turned around to see Jack on the left-hand side of the cave, near three large boulders.

'What've you found?' asked Sol.

'I'm not sure, but it could be ancient treasure from

pirates,' said Jack. 'There's some big wooden boxes, and this one's slightly open, so I can see inside.'

'Yeah, it's full of parcels of different sizes, but they're all wrapped up in a cloth material.'

'I wonder how long those boxes have been here.' I was thinking out loud.

'Can't tell,' said Jack. 'There's no dampness on the outside of the boxes and they're tucked up on these rocks out of the damp puddles we've been walking around in.'

Sol was now with Jack, inspecting the boxes.

'There's no way of knowing how long these have been here. I can't get a clue from the boxes either, there's no writing on them.'

'Perhaps this is a smugglers storage place,' I said. 'Do you think smugglers from the islands further west or south have delivered this stuff here, then some local smugglers from Pontus are responsible maybe, for moving it on to its next stage?'

'I think Sam was saying that ancient artefacts are taken from Mexico, and then go around to the east coast of the USA, towards Florida,' said Sol, 'because they can get more money for them up there.'

'Yes, that makes Pontus, about a halfway point in that journey,' I calculated.

'So how long will these boxes and parcels have been here?' Sol asked. 'Are they likely to be collecting them soon?'

'I don't know,' said Jack, 'but I don't want to be here

when the smugglers come back. I can't imagine they'd be very nice people to meet, somehow.'

'Someone might be on their way now, to collect it all,' Sol said. 'I think we need to get out of here and get back so we can report it to the police.'

'Perhaps we should open a few of these packets and see what's inside first,' I suggested. 'I don't believe the police would be interested in coming here unless they think it's valuable treasure.'

'Yeah, I reckon you're right, Lucy' said Jack, 'let's have a look at what's in these boxes. We might be able to identify some real treasure.'

'Perhaps just open one at first,' I said, 'but do it very carefully.'

'If the police do come here, I expect they'll do a stake-out and hide in the back of the cave waiting to catch them,' said Jack.

'Maybe,' I said nervously, 'but let's take a quick look at the packages, then get out of here before they come back.'

But our plan was stopped by what happened next!

'What's that noise?' I hissed.

I stopped talking, as a low rumbling noise starting to get closer and louder.

'Heck, what's happening?' asked Sol. 'It's too loud for thunder.'

'Yeah, and thunder wouldn't make the ground vibrate like this, either,' shouted Jack.

'Come on,' I urged. 'I think we need to get out of here. I can feel the earth moving under my feet.'

The crashing got louder. There was a sound of grinding rock. Dust blew up around the entrance to the cave and it suddenly got darker.

'I think we might be too late,' said Jack.

Sol had rushed across to the cave entrance. 'You'll not believe it,' he yelled back. 'It only took seconds, but we've now got large boulders blocking the entrance.'

I could hear his laboured breathing as he tried to push the rocks. Then he stopped and looked at where the entrance had been. 'They're too heavy for me to push away and I can't see any way through.'

The noise, vibrations and dust clouds had stopped.

Jack and I carefully made our way across the rocks to join Sol.

'You're right, Sol,' I said. I stared ahead of me, at where the cave entrance had been. It was so dark, hardly a shaft of light entered the cave and we were relying on our torches to see anything at all.

We all tried to push against the boulders which had fallen against the cave entrance, but despite heaving and shoving … the boulders didn't move. These boulders had obviously been loosened from their places above us on the hillside and had come tumbling down.

I remembered the sight of the cliff face when our aircraft

had flown over a few weeks ago on our trip to research the seagrass areas. Some places between the trees were white, showing the rock had fallen off and pushed all the trees out of the way as they fell.

'These rocks have probably been loosened by the constant movement of water from the waterfall above us,' I said.

'Well,' said Jack, 'it's great for Lucy to teach us all about why the rocks have just thrown themselves down the mountain, but the problem is ... we can't get out.'

All thoughts of investigating what Jack thought was pirate's treasure, had gone from my head. We now had a serious problem to solve.

'Heck,' I said, 'how do we get out of here and back to our boat?'

I knew I was asking a question that none of us could answer.

We were trapped.

CHAPTER TWENTY-THREE
Pitch Black

Light from our torches pierced the pitch-black darkness behind us. I pointed my torch so I could see both Jack and Sol's faces. Jack looked serious, but Sol looked very worried.

I had to admit I wasn't too happy either.

Jack started to take charge of the situation.

'We need to find another way out?' he said. 'We could try to find a way through the cave system. There might be a tunnel which will lead us out of here.'

I pulled myself together and started to think more clearly.

'Okay,' said Jack, 'are you both happy if I lead? We'll start at the back of this cave and see if we can see any light from afar, or maybe just the feeling of cold air coming in will help us.'

'I think we should tie ourselves together,' I said, 'then if one of us falls the other two can hold on to them and stop them slipping through a hole or something.'

'Good idea,' said Jack, 'we'll spread out, one behind the other.'

We found our rucksacks and Jack pulled out the rope.

'Thank goodness we thought of putting spare torch batteries in, too,' I said, 'we mustn't let ourselves be trapped without light. These rocks look treacherous, it would be so easy to slip and break an ankle. If we're in here for long we might even have to use just one torch at a time to save energy in the batteries.'

'I don't want to be in here for a long time,' said Sol. 'I want to find a way out as soon as possible. My brain keeps imagining me as a skeleton sitting on a rock, having died from starvation.'

'Don't be such a weed, Sol,' said Jack. 'We're not going to die in here.'

'Don't be too harsh, Jack,' I said. 'I'm not too comfortable about being trapped in here, either. At least Sol is telling us how he's feeling.'

'It's just that nobody knows exactly where we are,' said Sol, 'or that we're trapped, do they? How could anyone find us?'

'Yeah, sorry, Sol,' said Jack, sheepishly. 'I guess all three of us are not exactly happy about this situation, are we?'

'No, that's for sure,' I said. 'We definitely have a problem and it's up to us to get ourselves out of here. We have torches, a rope and some food and water, so it might not be too bad. Come on, let's get going and find an escape route.'

We tied ourselves together with the rope and Jack led the way, with me behind him and Sol at the back.

'At least my rucksack's not so heavy now we've taken the rope out,' said Jack.

We made our way across the slippery rocks towards the back of the cave. Jack used his right hand to feel for the wall of the cave and follow its route.

'Okay, we've found a way out of this cave, I think,' said Jack. Looks like there's another cave behind the first one.'

I swung my torch around to look further. The cave roof was quite a distance above me, and from the roof, there were structures hanging down, like needles. On the floor of the cave there were more needle like objects, this time pointing upwards.

'Look at these,' I said. 'I think they're cave structures known as stalactites. I've read about them and they take millions of years to form from water dripping down.'

I realised I was muttering out loud about some science I'd recently done at school on limestone rock and fossils.

'These cave walls are completely natural,' I explained, 'just hard limestone rock with tiny specks of sparking minerals where I'm shining my torch.'

Was I kidding myself that by keeping their minds occupied on their surroundings, both Jack and Sol would both stop worrying about our situation?

Neither of them had replied.

'I expect there'll be fossils of old sea creatures in these walls too,' I continued.

The floor was still slippery from the dampness and puddles.

'I am listening, Lucy,' said Sol, 'but if you don't mind, I'll keep looking at my feet, rather than the walls just at the moment. I think I need to concentrate on being careful and not slipping on these wet rocks. Perhaps you can give us a science lesson when we get out of here!'

'Yeah, sorry, Sol,' I said. 'Good point ... let's just concentrate on getting out of this dilemma first.'

CHAPTER TWENTY-FOUR
Which Way Now?

'I reckon I can smell fresh air this way,' said Jack.

'Can you see any light ahead,' I asked, 'like we could see in the sea cave?'

'No! It looks pretty dark,' said Jack. 'It looks like the tunnel's going to twist and turn and ahead of us it looks like we're going to have to start climbing, too. There are some big rocks ahead, but I can't see any other way to go.'

We followed Jack in a line as we wriggled our way through the tunnel.

Sol and I then stopped to watch Jack climbing up the boulders.

'We really need some of those old miner's headlight torches,' I said quietly to Sol, 'I've seen them in pictures. We'd be able to have the lights on our foreheads, and then both hands would be free to help us clamber through here.'

'They sound really good. I'll have to remember to put those on our list for next time we plan to get lost in a cave,' said Sol sarcastically.'

I started to giggle. 'Perhaps we could get someone to fit some stairs and handrails inside before we go in, too. That'd make it easier to climb,' I suggested.

'Great idea, Lucy,' said Sol, expanding on our silliness. 'We'll have to plan for all eventualities. D'you reckon you could have dogs trained up too, like they do for mountain rescues? They could sniff their way along and find an exit.'

We giggled quietly, so as not to disturb Jack's concentration on his climb.

'Sorry folks,' Jack called down, 'but I think you'll find this climb's gonna be fingernail stuff, gripping on wet rocks and trying not let yourself fall back down.'

We negotiated our first rocky boulder climb carefully by taking it slowly and waiting for each one of us to get to the top.

'So how old is this cave system?' asked Sol.

'Probably millions of years old.' I guessed.

'Do you think anyone's ever been inside the back of this cave, where we are?' Sol asked.

'Who knows,' said Jack. 'I think we might have been the first inside the underwater cave. We might be the first again, to investigate the back of all of this cave structure.'

'I'd rather like it if someone else had investigated in here before us,' I said, 'as that might mean there's going to be an exit up here somewhere.'

We moved on through the next section of the cave system.

'Hang on,' said Jack, 'it's suddenly getting very narrow. I'll go through first and then stand by to help you, Lucy and then you help Sol.'

Jack took off his rucksack and passed it to me.

I watched as he contorted his body into strange shapes so he could get through the tight, limited space.

If Jack could get through the hole, I thought, then Sol and I would be able to manage it. Jack was more muscular that either Sol or me.

Jack eventually squeezed through the hole, and I pushed his rucksack through after him.

Then it was my turn. I couldn't believe how small the space was. I had to lie on my stomach, then push on my legs to wriggle my way through.

Sol then began his journey through the tiny gap, but he was skinny and smaller than either Jack or me, so it seemed easier for him.

We continued to clamber upwards.

'I think I can see a bit of light ahead,' Jack shouted.

We continued to follow along behind him, getting higher and higher through the mountain cave tunnel.

'Yes,' yelled Jack from ahead of us. 'There is a kind of hole ahead and now there's lots of light coming in.'

Jack had reached the end of the cave tunnel and was stretching himself out on his stomach and creeping carefully towards the edge.

He looked downwards. 'Heck, there's a big drop out here and it seems to go downwards for ever. We don't want to fall down there.' Then he turned and looked upwards.

'No, it's okay, there's daylight up there. That'll be the way out. But I haven't got a clue how we're supposed to get up there.'

We took turns to lie at the edge of the tunnel.

When it was my turn, I looked at our next challenge.

Our tunnel had emerged on the side of a circular vertical column which was made of brick. It was about half my height across and there was nothing below us but a deep, dark void. I wasn't tall enough to reach out across to the other side without losing my present, safe position. I'd end up falling down into the dark never-ending space below.

'Well, the bricks mean it's man-made,' I said, 'and it seems to go upwards towards the outside world.' By laying on my back and poking my head through the hole I could see upwards.

'I can see clouds and blue sky,' I exclaimed. Relief spread through my body as I saw the sky above. 'This is a way out but I've no idea how we're supposed to climb up a sheer vertical wall. It's not that far up to the surface but if we fell, we'd probably die.'

'There's no ladder and as it's not a natural rock wall where there are no cracks and hand holes. We'd never manage to climb up there. It's just smooth bricks all the way up and no hand-holds at all.'

Sol took a look.

'We've managed to nearly rescue ourselves,' said Sol, 'but I can't see how we'll ever manage to climb up a vertical brick chamber like this one.'

'You're right. We've got close to finding our way out,' I said, 'but this bit looks impossible.'

CHAPTER TWENTY-FIVE
Is Anybody There?

I was resting at the edge of the tunnel, trying to figure out how we could climb up and finally escape from the cave system.

The sky and scudding clouds looked close yet we had no way of getting any nearer to the surface. Our tunnel had come out to this brick column at an angle of 90o. My brain was swirling … but there wasn't an easy answer.

Then I heard a voice.

'Albert, Charlie … here boys. Come on.'

I knew that voice. I signed with relief and turned my head so I could shout up towards the tall brick hole.

I cupped my hands and shouted at the top of my voice.

'Ellen, Ellen … is that you? ELLEN, we're down here. ELLEN!'

'Who's that?' I heard her voice again. 'Where's that voice coming from?'

'Quick, all of us shout together,' I said to Jack and Sol.

'Ellen, it's us,' yelled Jack.

'Down here,' yelled Sol.

'Ellen, Ellen,' I called.

Then we saw her. Her ginger hair and freckly face appeared over the edge at the top.

'Is anybody there?' she called.

'Yes, it's us,' I called back. 'We're all here, Jack, Sol and me, Lucy.'

'What the heck are you three doing down my well?' she gasped.

'A well, of course,' I said. 'A well explains the shape of this structure.'

It now all made sense. Our tunnel had emerged into the side of the old brick well in Ellen's garden high up on Pirates' Peak.

'Ellen, can you help get us out?' I yelled.

'We were investigating the cave and got trapped,' called Jack.

'Okay, I can see you now. I never realised there was a connection to a cave down there. You've got to be careful though. This well is incredibly deep. Careful you don't slip out from where you're safe at the moment. If you fall down, you'd probably kill yourselves.'

'Do you have a rope or something?' asked Sol.

'Mmm! Let me think about this. Hang on ... I'll only be a few minutes,' said Ellen, as she disappeared.

'That's okay,' said Jack, 'we can hang on... we're not going anywhere.'

For the first time since the rocks came down onto the entrance of the cave, Jack was smiling.

Sol and I relaxed too and exchanged hi-fives.

'Well, we're safe,' I said, 'although we've still got to get up to Ellen's garden. At least someone knows where we are now.'

It must've been over ten minutes before Ellen returned. I heard her telling the dogs to move out of her way. Then her head appeared above us again.

'Right, I've been inside the back of my shed and got all my old rock-climbing gear out.'

'What!' I gasped, 'you climb up mountains too?'

Jack and Sol burst out laughing.

'Well, I'm not surprised,' said Sol, 'she is Ellen ... isn't she? She hasn't always been old and we know in the past she's been a diver, and she can fly a plane.'

Ellen ignored my question as she seemed to be bending down and untangling some ropes. She then threw one of the ropes down the well.

'Right,' announced Ellen. 'Here's the plan. I've secured ropes around a solid tree, here in the garden and I've attached my rope through the descender I've clipped to my harness. It means I can abseil down the well. I'll then be able to bring you up, one at a time.'

She was wearing a harness and had a bright yellow helmet on her head. I watched as she sat on the top of the brick wall of the well, adjusting her ropes. She put all her body weight on the rope to support herself, then turned to face into the bricks, with her feet pushing her body away from the wall. She gradually leant back and started to descend, allowing a small quantity of rope through the gadgets tied to her harness.

I noticed she was wearing tight fingerless gloves and little boots that seemed to stick to the bricks as she steadied herself downwards.

Within minutes she'd come down far enough to be level with our tunnel exit.

CHAPTER TWENTY-SIX
Back to the Surface.

'Right, you first, Lucy,' said Ellen. She had stopped her descent and was hanging in the middle of the well. She unclipped the spare harness from her belt and passed it to me.

'Just clamber into that,' she said, 'I'll check you've got it on properly, and then I'll clip you onto the rope with me. I've got a pulley system attached so I can get you up to the top.'

I looked at her equipment and couldn't see how we could possibly climb up using such thin rope.

Ellen saw my frowns and reassured me.

'No, it's okay, Lucy,' she said, 'the pulley system does all the work. It'll be a bit slower going up than it was for me to come down, but we'll get up there eventually.'

'You're tying very fancy knots,' I said, watching how her old fingers smoothly controlled the rope.

Clunk, the rope from my harness was now connected to Ellen. I now had to take a leap of faith from the cave tunnel to the middle of nowhere.

I put my weight on the rope attached to my harness and pushed off with my feet.

'Phew! That wasn't fun,' I said, as I hung in mid-air, 'that was scary!'

'You'll be okay now. I'll soon get you to the top,' Ellen reassured me.

'Hang around, boys. I'll be back down for you in a moment,' said Ellen.

Jack was laughing again.

'I'll be back' said Jack in a deep, rustic American accent, 'sounds like a film-script!'

Now Sol was laughing too. 'It's okay, Ellen,' replied Sol. 'We can wait!'

Ellen worked the pulley, and she and I went upwards as the rope slid through the equipment with the brake securing us and stopping us from falling downwards.

I clambered out at the top of the well. Charley and Albert saw me and ran across, jumping up at me.

'Steady, you two,' I said, pushing the two hairy dogs away from me, 'you'll push me back down the well if you're not careful.'

CHAPTER TWENTY-SEVEN
Remote Control

I untied my rope from Ellen's harness and watched as she quickly went back down for Sol.

'Okay, here's another one,' said Ellen, as she arrived back at the surface with Sol clipped on to her.

'Ellen, will you be able to manage Jack?' I asked. 'He's a bit heavier than Sol and me.'

'Mmm, that's a thought, Lucy.' Ellen clambered out of the well.

'I think I've got an idea,' she said.

She unclipped her harness and went into the house.

'I'll use the old Defender,' she said, rattling some car keys.

A few minutes later she had backed her old Land Rover Defender close to the well.

She went around to the rear of the vehicle where I saw her connect a winch to the tow hitch. Then she attached her harness to the winch and made sure her abseil rope was still attached as a back-up.

'Well, this may not be the way the mountain rescue people would do it,' she said, 'but I think it'll work to get Jack up here with us.'

'I'll go and get young Mr Muscles now,' said Ellen, 'you're right he's much heavier than you two.'

I watched as she put her helmet and harness back on and double-checked all the knots in the equipment.

She slipped back into the well, and this time I could hear a whirring sound and saw the winch letting out the rope as she descended.

'I think she's got a remote control for the winch,' said Sol. 'That is so cool!'

A couple of minutes later, we saw the winch reverse its direction and start pulling the rope back up.

'Here we are,' said Ellen as she popped up at the top of the well.

Sol and I helped her to climb over the lip of the well then helped Jack to climb out. He had been hanging below Ellen but was still attached to her abseiling gear.

'That was really, great,' said Jack. 'Thank you so much Ellen, you've been a real star.'

'No problem,' said Ellen, 'it's the equipment that does the work.'

'I can't believe you know how to do all this stuff,' said Jack.

'Learn something new every day, that's what I say,' said Ellen. 'I learnt to do this years ago. You don't forget how to do things, you know. I haven't done any abseiling for years, but it all seemed to come back to me, alright.'

We helped her untie the rope from the tree and put the equipment back in her shed.

'I think I'll phone Dan and ask him to come up here and drive you back home,' said Ellen. 'I must admit, I'm feeling a bit weary, after all that.'

We were soon sitting on Ellen's balcony, looking out to sea and drinking cold sodas as we waited for Dan.

'I can't believe how you all got yourselves into such a pickle,' said Ellen.

I told her about the cave in the rainforest at the bottom of Pirates' Peak, then the rock fall and how we were trapped. I explained our long climb upwards inside the tunnels.

'Then we suddenly ended up here … under your house,' I said.

'Oh, my goodness,' said Ellen, 'what an adventure!'

'Uncle Dan's gonna be pretty cross with us though, isn't he?' said Jack. 'We've left his boat back down on the beach. I think we're going to be in real trouble with him for that.'

'Well, it wasn't our fault that the cave entrance got blocked was it?' said Sol. 'We didn't mean to get ourselves into this situation.'

'No,' I said, 'but we told him we were going fishing and having a picnic on a nearby beach. We didn't tell him we were going to leave his boat to look after itself and search for a cave system. Hopefully, when Ellen speaks to him, he'll stay calm.'

'Maybe,' said Ellen, 'but he'll be worrying and thinking about how he's going to tell your Mum you've been in danger again, Lucy. He hates it when your Mum thinks he's not been looking after you.'

'We got away with our dive into the cave,' I said, 'but I think we're going to be in deep trouble with Dan this time for borrowing his boat, and not telling him exactly where we were planning to go.'

'Yep,' said Sol, 'and don't forget Dan's boat is down there on the beach, at the bottom of Pirates' Peak now, with nobody looking after it.'

'If someone's stolen the RIB,' said Jack, 'we'll never be allowed to borrow a boat, ever again.'

CHAPTER TWENTY-EIGHT
All Out?

'How do you three get yourselves into so much trouble?' asked Dan.

Within minutes of him arriving, Ellen had replenished the drinks and biscuits in front of us, and Jack, Sol and myself explained again how we'd found the cave ... and how the rock fall had not been our fault. We described the trip through the tunnels and Sol emphasised how careful we'd been on the slippery rocks, and then our delight when we'd heard Ellen's voice.

'I reckon you three, have scrapped through all this by the skin of your teeth,' said Dan. 'You could've been in real trouble here.'

I didn't move my head, but just by quick eye movements, I exchanged looks with Sol and Jack. I raised my eyebrows. Had we got away with it? Was Dan angry with us or not?

'Yes,' said Ellen, 'we could get annoyed about the fact that no-one knew exactly where you were, and I suppose if you'd not found a way out of the cave system it'd be a different story, but you planned your adventure well, you thought of torches and had a rope tied to you all as you worked your way through the tunnels.'

I started to relax.

'Actually, Dan,' said Ellen, 'when you look back on this, I reckon they've done pretty well.'

Dan sat quietly, deep in thought.

Had Ellen stood up for us enough? Was there going to be a 'BUT'?

I looked at Sol and Jack again, I could see none of us were sure of what Dan's final reaction was going to be.

We soon found out.

'It's all very well, Ellen,' said Dan, shaking his head, 'yes, this time they did find a way out … BUT we had no way of knowing where they were. They'd not told us their plans. If they hadn't found their way through the tunnels, they'd have been there for ever … we'd never have found them. We would've had no idea where to look for them.'

I looked down at my feet. It felt like we were in real trouble with Dan.

'I'm pretty cross with all three of you for not letting us know where you were going,' said Dan.

I decided that a quick apology might be useful.

'Actually, Dan's right,' I said, quickly. 'If we'd not found the way out, we could have been trapped in the cave and no-one knew where we were. I'm really sorry, Dan.'

Jack and Sol were nodding. None of us were smiling anymore.

'Dan, I promise you,' I said, 'we'll never plan to go somewhere like this again without telling people where we're going first.'

Sol and Jack continued to nod.

'Yes, Uncle Dan,' said Jack, 'I'm sorry. I'll always talk to you first in future.'

'Yeah, me too,' said Sol, 'to be honest I was pretty scared when we got trapped.'

'We know you're right, Dan,' I said, 'we might never have been found. We could have ended up eventually as skeletons in there.'

CHAPTER TWENTY-NINE
Anger

I thought back to the previous day. Unfortunately, our apologies to Dan were not enough for us to be forgiven easily.

Once Dan realised that we'd left the RIB on the beach under Pirates' Peak, thunder clouds formed over his head. He was in a terrible mood. He drove us back to Jude's Bay moaning all the way.

I had to explain to Mum what had happened, and she agreed with every word Dan said about dishonesty. She even told me off for upsetting Dan so much. I was now in trouble at home too.

Dan was still smouldering the following morning. We tried to steer clear of him, but it was impossible.

Jack received the full force of Dan's anger when the three of us arrived at the Dive Centre the next morning.

'And you, Jack ... you lied to me about where you were going. Going fishing, you said. Well that wasn't true, was it?'

Dan stopped looking directly at Jack and swung around to include Sol and myself. I'd never seen him so angry.

'If you're going to borrow things like the RIB ... you at least owe me the decency of a proper explanation. No, you all lied and you're all banned from using the RIB again.'

He stormed out of the equipment room.

'I think we need to stay out of Dan's way,' said Jack.

We quickly finished getting the equipment ready for the students' afternoon dive and headed for Drifters.

'Let's go and find Joel,' I said. 'I hope he's not angry with us too.'

Joel was actually a bit sheepish. 'I suppose I encouraged you kids too much. All them tales of pirates' treasure back in the old days. Yep, I can understand why Dan's so cross but I don't really think it's because he reckons he could have lost the RIB. He's probably upset 'cos you kids were in danger and he didn't know where you was and what you was getting' up too. No, you three had better be on yer best behaviour for a while. The storm'll pass. You all keeps yer heads down for a while. Be helpful around the Dive Centre as usual. I'm sure he'll let you go off by yourselves again soon. Just let him calm down a bit first.'

Dan was driving the Dive Boat. He had eight students on board, plus Jack, Sol and me. We were heading for Pirates' Peak beach to collect the RIB before we went diving.

Dan started repeating his arguments again and we had nowhere to hide.

'That RIB cost me a lot of money,' he was saying, 'and you left it on a beach where anyone could've stolen it.'

I was scared of what we'd find when we got there. What would Dan be like if we got there, and found the RIB had been stolen?

When Dan saw where we'd hidden the RIB in the trees, he had to admit it was well concealed.

I started to breathe normally again. I could feel my body relaxing as a sense of relief rushed through me.

'I can't see it easily,' said Dan, 'although I know it's there somewhere. Okay, you did your best to look after the RIB, I suppose, but I'm not letting you all off the hook yet. I need to feel I can trust you.'

Dan took the Dive Boat as close as he could to the small beach, then sent Jack, Sol and me to swim ashore and retrieve the RIB.

Just a day earlier we'd carefully laid the leaves across the boat, but now we dragged them off quickly and discarded them.

We took hold of the handles around the top cushioned surface of the rubber boat and hauled it over the sand and back into the water.

Sol didn't bother to start the engine as the Dive Boat was so close, so we used the spare paddles to manoeuvre it, threw a rope to Dan and clambered back onboard the larger vessel. I made sure the RIB was firmly tied to the stern.

'Well, at least the boat was still there,' said Dan, 'and we've got it back safe and sound. Now, let's take these students for a dive.'

CHAPTER THIRTY
Students and Shoals

We fell into our normal duties. Sol, as boat captain whilst Dan was underwater, and Jack and I checking the students carefully, ensuring they all had their air switched on, and hoses connected properly.

'I can't wait to get underwater,' said Jack, as we watched the last of the students disappear below the waves.

'Why?' I asked, worrying if he was too hot or maybe wasn't feeling well. 'Are you alright?'

'Yeah, I'm fine ... just thinking it'll be quieter down there, without Dan grumbling at us all the time. My ears are hurting so much, I can't wait.'

I turned to Sol behind me, 'Enjoy your peace and quiet, Sol,' I said.

'Sure,' he smiled. 'Have a good dive. Next time it'll be Jack's turn to look after the boat, so I can dive instead.'

'Hey, Lucy, sounds like Sol wants to get wet,' said Jack, laughing, 'let's try for a record-breaking splash-in. We can go in at the same time from both corners of the stern of the boat. We'll make the boat rock and we might get Sol wet!'

We lined up in our positions, still laughing.

'On three,' said Jack, 'ONE-TWO-THREE!'

We splashed fins first into the sea at the same time.

From below the surface I looked up and could see the boat rocking. We'd find out later if Sol had got wet!

We followed the students down to eighteen metres and were immediately surrounded by a shoal of blue fusiliers. I loved swimming through such a large mass of fish ... they didn't worry about us at all. We knew they couldn't hurt us either. They stayed grouped together, moving around us as they swam. The long black lines along the middle of the sides of their bodies were edged with flashes of silver. Each fish watched the black lines of its neighbours and, as the shoal moved through the water, if some of them started to move to the left, they would all move, and then back again depending on what dangers were ahead.

I watched, fascinated as fish around the edge of the shoal changed places with those in the middle. They all took turns to be safe. I wondered if any of them ever noticed if a larger fish came up to the outside of the group and ate one of them?

The fish seemed constantly aware of dangers, yet somehow knew that Jack, Sol and I presented them with no risk at all. They just adjusted their positions as they swam around us.

I wished I'd brought the video camera with me that Ellen had lent us. Being amongst this stunning throng of silver fish, glinting in the sun shining down from above, was incredibly peaceful and relaxing. It would be good to record it and let Mum see the beauty of the underwater environment.

My Mum had still not learnt to dive, despite both Dan and I trying to get her involved.

It was an uneventful dive as the students were now becoming more skilled, and Jack was right, it was good to be underwater where we couldn't hear Dan's voice moaning about our behaviour.

Back aboard the dive boat less than an hour later, Jack and I joked with Sol about trying to get him wet.

'Sorry, guys,' said Sol, 'good try, but you only made the boat move a bit. I stayed completely dry! I decided I'd won the competition though and awarded myself an extra bit of cake.'

'Better be some left for us,' said Jack, smiling.

Dan gathered the students around him whilst Jack and I tidied up the equipment.

'That was an excellent dive,' Dan said. 'You're all showing improvement and confidence in the water now. Well, done everyone.'

Sol started the engine and headed back towards the jetty at Dolphin Beach.

I handed round Mum's homemade cake. Everyone had their mouths full, including Jack, when he looked up, pointed out to sea and shouted.

'Hey, look over there.' he yelled, spitting cake crumbs from his mouth all over the place.

He was pointing towards a fishing boat ahead of us. The crew were waving … but it didn't look like the friendly sort of wave we often exchanged with boats as we passed by.

No, this was a wave for help! These fishermen needed us to come over … there was obviously something wrong, they were in trouble in some way or another … and they urgently needed our help.

CHAPTER THIRTY-ONE
Helping the Fishermen

As we approached the fishing boat, I could see two men on the deck. Dan took our boat alongside and Sol and I helped to throw ropes and attach the two boats together.

'What's your problem?' Dan called across to them.

'We've got a net around our propeller,' the shorter of the two men was speaking. 'We can't start our engine and we've been drifting around for about an hour now.'

Dan clambered from one boat to the other, asking questions about the problem.

'Start getting our dive kit ready, Lucy,' Dan called across to me. 'We can take dive knives and cut the net away. It shouldn't take us too long.'

I took our dive jackets and attached them to two full tanks of air, then struggled back into my wetsuit. It was always more difficult to put on a damp wetsuit than a dry one.

Within a few minutes, Dan and I had entered the water to inspect the propeller. It didn't take long to understand the problem.

Our eyes saw a tangled mess of netting. Green plastic netting! We took separate sides and used our sharp knives to cut the netting away. We both took care to cut it carefully. We didn't want to hack away at it and turn it into lots of small pieces. It needed it to come away in one large piece so we could get it onto the boat and take it back to land for disposal. It wasn't an easy task and it took us nearly half an hour before we surfaced, holding onto the netting very carefully.

The two fishermen took the net and tied it to their boat as Dan and I swam back to the dive boat.

Enrico, the owner of the boat started his engine and turned to thank us, but we were aghast at his next action.

He untied the cut net and threw it back into the ocean.

'No!' I yelled, 'don't do that. It'll get caught around dolphins and other sea creatures.'

Enrico shrugged his shoulders. 'Nah, I don't see no problem,' he said, 'lots of room in the ocean for all that stuff.'

I was fuming. There was no chance Dan and I could get back in the water in time to stop the heavy net descending. The net by now would have sunk further than the depth we could safely dive.

'You idiot,' shouted Dan, angrily, 'that plastic net is going to remain in the ocean for hundreds of years and will endanger the lives of thousands of sea creatures.'

'We'll report you,' I yelled, although I didn't know who I'd report it too.

Dan was angry, shaking his fist at the fisherman.

'You're being stupid and selfish,' he yelled. 'That's appalling behaviour. D'you know, I wouldn't have charged you for my help, but now ... I'm going to send you a whacking great bill. We should have left you and your boat to drift and smash against the rocks.'

The captain shrugged and turned away and the crewman released the ropes which had tied our two boats together. Their engine was put in gear and they chugged away from us.

Dan and I looked at each other.

'I can't believe what just happened,' I said. 'We need laws to stop that sort of behaviour, and that awful man should be fined for what he's done. I'd go to court and give evidence right now, if I could.'

'Yes, and I'd join you, Lucy,' said Dan, 'people like that shouldn't be allowed to get away with polluting the ocean.'

'What we need is some sort of system,' I said, 'to make sure the fishermen know how to behave. We need to ensure that behaviour doesn't keep happening.'

'I think you need to go and talk to the Mayor again,' Dan said, looking at me. 'You'll be able to talk about what can be done.'

CHAPTER THIRTY-TWO
Sombre Mood

I was in a sombre mood as the boat arrived back at the pontoon on Dolphin Beach and we all headed for Drifter's.

I was also starving after all my physical efforts of diving and then cutting away the rope from the propeller. I definitely needed food.

As we approached the restaurant, I saw Joel and Mum sitting at a table outside, chatting quietly.

'You'll never guess what happened,' I started to speak. Words came out of my mouth so quickly.

'Hey, young lady,' Joel said, 'slow down. What's all the fuss about?'

After Dan and I had told the story of the fisherman and the plastic net, Joel and Mum could understand why we were so upset.

'You're right, Lucy,' said Mum, 'there really should be fines for this sort of thing. You've already experienced how netting can harm dolphins, haven't you? You need to talk to the Mayor of St. Stephens again, as soon as possible. These men shouldn't get away with such awful behaviour.'

'They's so many problems with fishermen,' said Joel, with a big sigh. 'They's catch too many fish or use the wrong sized nets. Then there's 'em fishermen who use trawling equipment right down on the seabed. Trawling is a terrible way of treating the home of so many creatures. They's kill lots of creatures with 'em trawling machines being dragged over the seabed.'

Dan phoned Ellen and asked her to help plan a meeting with the Mayor of St. Stephens, to stop to the fishermen's bad habits.

Ellen and I had worked with the Mayor before and successfully had projects accepted to educate people about sea creatures and for systems to be put in place to stop litter getting into the sea. The litter problem on the island had certainly improved.

Dan thought it was great when the Mayor had asked us to be his 'eyes' in the oceans. The Mayor knew divers could see what was happening in the ocean in close up, which of course, the politicians couldn't do.

'You should get Dan to give you some diving lessons,' I'd said to the Mayor one day, 'and let you see the problems for yourself.'

The Mayor had laughed loudly and told me he felt more comfortable staying on land and ensuring the administration of the Island was working properly.

'I'll leave it to you, young 'uns to do the diving and keep me informed,' he'd said. 'I mean it though, Lucy, I need to hear from you about any problems you come across, so we can keep this island as ocean-friendly as possible.'

I reminded Dan of my conversation with the Mayor.

'The Mayor doesn't need to be a diver to understand the problem of throwing a large plastic net into the sea,' said

Dan. 'Do you know, I still can't believe I actually saw someone do that.'

I sat quietly next to Dan, whilst Mum was in the restaurant ordering our meal.

'Dan, I was wondering whether Mum is ready to learn to dive, yet,' I said.

'I don't know,' said Dan, 'so far I've only managed to get her swimming.'

Jack and Sol could hear our conversation.

'I can't imagine living here and not being able to dive,' said Jack.

'When you first arrived here on Pontus, your Mum was determined she would never learn to dive,' said Dan, 'but she might've changed her mind now she can swim. I've not mentioned it to her for a while, but I'll try again.'

'Maybe she'll learn to dive, then come out on the dive boat, with us,' I said. 'Don't you think that would be a great idea?'

'Yes,' said Joel, 'we needs to help her, get her more involved in the island life.'

Jack and Sol exchanged a whisper.

Jack was smiling, and nudged Sol to speak.

'Yeah, we reckon that'd be great,' said Sol, 'cos your Mum might bring more cake on board the boat, too.'

CHAPTER THIRTY-THREE

Planning

'It's all about education, again, isn't it?' said Ellen. She was eating a Drifters' 'Fish of the Day' platter for her evening meal.

'These fishermen don't know enough about how to protect sea life. Crazy really, as their job is to catch fish and sell it … but they don't seem to understand how to protect fish stocks. Catching fish which are too small to eat is such a waste. There will be no fish left in the sea if this carries on.'

'There's already a problem with all the plastic in the oceans,' said Joel, shaking his head. 'I'd heard someone say there's gonna be more plastic in the sea than there are fish in fifty years' time, an' that's a terrible thought.'

'Aren't there rules for the whole world about protecting all the different species of fish?' I asked, 'or is it up to every country, or island nation like Pontus … to make up their own rules?'

'There are international laws.' said Ellen. 'Usually they've been agreed by the United Nations, but the problem comes when individual fishermen might not have heard of those rules.'

Ellen started telling us about Fishery Protection Officers in other countries and the need for boats to patrol the fishing areas around Pontus.

'We need to tell the Mayor about the importance of

licensing,' she said, 'and taking those licences away if fishermen aren't following the rules … a bit like Lucy, Jack and Sol having had their use of the RIB taken away from them.'

I looked across at Jack and his head was drooping. The three of us were still sore about that decision.

'Thanks, Ellen,' said Jack, 'I'm really pleased you reminded me of that. I keep thinking about those packages back in the cave. We still haven't had a chance to get back there. We still don't know if we were right in thinking it was smuggled treasure.'

Our conversation was interrupted as I saw a familiar figure walking across the sand towards us.

'Tom,' I yelled, 'you're back, it's great to see you.'

I gave him a big hug.

Tom was a friend, who Jack, Sol and I had originally thought was a total baddie. However, we soon realised we had completely misunderstood him. Tom was really a young businessman who'd had made a fortune from an internet game when he was still a teenager and he was now using his money and connections to help other people. He was now helping to organise marine experts to build the marine park areas around Pontus as well as design a Turtle Rescue Centre that we'd planned too. Tom really was a hero, as he'd been working away from the island to secure the finances for both these important schemes.

Tom announced that all his work was done with financing

our schemes and he'd come back to have a few days relaxation.

'Protection officers and boats. Good ideas.' said Tom. 'Now that I've sorted out the finances for the Marine Park and Turtle Centre, I can offer to help the Mayor with getting finance for the cost of a patrol boat, and I can organise the jobs for the officers and their training quite quickly.'

'So, that's what the mayor needs to address then, isn't it,' I said, 'some sort of Fisheries Protection team, to educate people about the sea creatures and to fine fishermen if they get it wrong ... that should stop their bad fishing habits, such as overfishing or doing what they did this morning ... throwing their nets into the ocean. Fisherman need to know of and obey the rules.'

'Let's think about what you need to say to the mayor,' said Dan, 'who's taking notes?'

Mum raised a finger.

'Me, again,' she said, 'I'll write down all the useful ideas we have, then Ellen and Lucy can see the Mayor after school on Monday.'

My brain cells suddenly had a 'double loop-the-loop, light-flashing' moment. What if I got Mum involved with the meetings with the Mayor?

My mouth took over and I heard myself talking.

'If you're making notes, Mum, then perhaps you should come with Ellen and me and help us explain everything?'

'Would that be alright?' she said, 'I can get time off work

for something this important and it's only a short walk to the Council offices next-door from where I work. Yes, I'd love to come with you.'

I exchanged a fist-bump with Jack when Mum couldn't see us.

'Let's get Mum on the team,' I said, quietly, then her next step might be to learn to dive?

'Actually, I think Tom should come with us to see the Mayor, too,' I suggested.

'That's a great idea,' said Sol. 'He knows how to find out things and make connections with people who the Mayor possibly doesn't know.'

'Yes, some of the things we've been talking about are affecting all places around the world, aren't they,' agreed Jack, 'it's not just about Pontus Island.'

'Tom, could you come tomorrow too?' I asked, 'and help us plan with the Mayor what we might be able to do about the fishing boats?'

Tom laughed, put his arm around my shoulders and gave me a squeeze. 'Well, nothing much has changed whilst I've been away, has it? You're still trying to get the world to look after the oceans, aren't you, Lucy?'

He looked around the group. 'I'm happy to be involved if that's okay with everyone else?'

We all nodded.

'I'll come then, if you think I can help you. I've enjoyed

everything I've done with you all previously ... no, bring it on. Let's go and fight another battle for all of Lucy's fishy friends.'

Mum then suggested we spend time researching the fishing rules before we met up with the Mayor again, so we arranged for Jack and Sol to come with me to the Community Library, where Mum worked, straight after school.

The next day Tom was there waiting for us and it was then we all first learned about supertrawlers. What we read that afternoon was horrifying!

CHAPTER THIRTY-FOUR
Supertrawlers

'Around the world,' quoted Jack, from an internet news article, 'in almost every part of the oceans, there are enormous fishing boats, as large as factories. These supertrawlers are destroying the seabeds around the world, and devastating fish stocks.'

'That sounds awful,' said Sol.

Tom was making notes. 'What's different about these big boats?' he asked.

I started reading out loud from my computer screen, which was showing a different article from the one on Jack's screen. 'Old methods of fishing around the world was to use special nets to catch small amounts of fish each time,' I quoted. 'This leaves enough fish in the sea for breeding and increasing the stocks again.'

Tom was listening attentively.

'It's different with these supertrawlers,' said Jack, 'these new boats are using enormous nets which scoop up everything. The nets catch, not just the fish which can be used as food supplies, but they also catch dolphins, mantas, turtles and everything which lives in the blue waters around the world.'

Jack stopped and looked up. 'This sounds terrible,' he said, then started reading again. 'With the catch in their enormous nets, everything is pulled on board the vast ship and within minutes everything in the nets is dead. The supertrawlers are constructed like vast factories, so a large catch from a sardine shoal can be separated within minutes from all the other species of fish, then be cleaned and canned ready to go straight to the supermarkets when the trawler eventually comes back to land.'

'The supertrawlers also catch marine creatures they can't sell. These are called 'by-catch'. All the by-catch dies and all these dead creatures get thrown back into the sea.'

'Oh no! It gets worse,' continued Jack. 'The supertrawlers use nets in the open water but they also have seabed trawling equipment, which act like giant farm machinery ploughing up a farmer's field. The trawling equipment is destroying all life on the seabed. Everything gets scooped up and killed.'

'So,' said Sol, 'whenever the supertrawlers come through an area of sea, then all the sea life is decimated, killing whole shoals catching both big and small fish and leaving nothing in the sea to continue to breed and grow?'

'Correct,' I said, 'that's exactly what's happening. These supertrawlers are clearing the sea of all marine life and harming the oceans forever. Once these fish species are all killed, there will be no more. Within a few years, these trawlers will have killed all life in nearly every ocean in the world.'

'This is appalling,' said Tom. 'Why are Governments around the world, allowing this to happen?'

I couldn't believe what I was learning. 'This is shocking.

This isn't just about fishermen throwing plastic nets back into the ocean. This is a threat to all marine life, everywhere around the world! How many people know about this?' I asked.

I felt the anger overflowing in my blood. My blood vessels wanted to burst. I could feel my face turning red.

'Why aren't people stopping this awful industry. There's so much damage been done already?'

I might be starting a conversation with the local Mayor in a few hours' time, but I felt I should be climbing a mountain and shouting from the very, very top ... shouting to everyone in the world.

'Stop supertrawlers ... before it's too late. Stop them. STOP THEM NOW!'

CHAPTER THIRTY-FIVE
Local Fishing Laws

Talking with the Mayor always seemed so easy. He was a relaxed, laid back Caribbean man who took life slowly. But although he spoke at a snail's pace, his brain acted quickly. He was listening carefully, and I was sure he was taking everything we were saying deeply into his thoughts. He would always wait before he spoke, as if he had considered every word before he actually said anything.

'So,' he said, 'we need Fishery Protection Officers and a patrol boat for them, that'll be the start. Strangely, I've been hearing from the mayors of some of the other islands near here, that they're investing money in this sort of protection too.'

'How about, if I volunteer to source a patrol boat?' said Tom. 'You can leave that to me.'

Tom outlined his ideas for financing a patrol boat and also to pay for new protection officers to be trained to do the job.

The mayor was beaming with delight. He'd appreciated Tom's previous support for Pontus Island, when he used some of his internet millions to invest money in building hotels. These were now bringing in more tourism and giving jobs to local people. All Tom's work on Pontus had helped the economy of the island.

'Well, that's great, Tom,' said the Mayor, smiling a very broad smile. 'I can assure you, that I will be looking into the rest of the problems. I will do everything I can to educate the fisherman, so they know all the local laws. And if we don't have enough laws, then

WE'LL MAKE UP SOME MORE,'

he slammed his fist down on his desk which made me jump. He was laughing out loud now, with a deep throaty noise coming from his mouth.

As he calmed down, he looked seriously at me.

'I'll be happy,' he said, 'to get everyone on this island to understand the importance of our beautiful oceans.'

'Thank you, Mr. Mayor,' I said, 'Everyone will benefit in the end. If the fishermen aren't more careful then all the stocks of fish will be destroyed by overfishing. If there's no fish in our local seas, then all the local restaurants will have nothing to serve their customers and the tourists won't have anything to eat either,' I said.

The mayor was nodding. 'Yep, we have to look after them fish properly, don't we?'

But I wasn't finished. The finances had been organised for our marine parks, and the Turtle Centre. We now had Tom supporting the expenses for the Fishery Protection boats and officers to protect the local waters around Pontus Island, and we had the Mayor writing new laws ... but I wanted to change the world! Change the world's understanding of the delicate state of the marine environment everywhere. Most of the human population now understood the terrible effects of plastics in the oceans, but who knew about supertrawlers?

'Can you get together with all the other mayors on the other islands to make laws about the supertrawlers, too?' I asked. 'We need to stop them from destroying the seabed and change their overfishing methods or it will destroy all sea life forever. What is needed is for all the islands to ban the big supertrawlers from being in the Caribbean, altogether! Local fishermen need to be able to catch fish properly, but we also need to protect all the oceans around here ... and supertrawlers do so much damage, they shouldn't be allowed to exist.'

'As always, Lucy,' said the Mayor, 'you make a great argument for what you believe in. Yes, of course I'll do my best to protect our seas and this time I'll enlist the help of all the other islands too. Together we'll have a much more powerful voice to argue for these supertrawlers to be totally outlawed.'

Mum and I exchanged a glance. Was she thinking the same thing as me? I was so pleased with the Mayor's reaction.

'There's a Caribbean Island Summit Meeting arranged to take place in a couple of weeks,' said the Mayor. 'It's a meeting of all the Governors and Mayors from all the islands and it's being held here on Pontus. I'll talk to the organisers and get them to put a discussion on supertrawlers on the agenda.'

'If you can tell everyone at that meeting,' I said, 'it'll be great.'

'I reckon you can talk about it better than me,' said the Mayor. 'Lucy, will you come and speak to the meeting. Then we'll be sure that everyone understands the problem.'

'Yes, of course I will,' I said, straight away.

After all, I'd spoken to my school, then I talked to all the councillors here on Pontus. Surely, it would only be a little step up to talk to Mayors from the other Islands.

I looked at Mum. She was smiling. 'Yes, Lucy, you can do it,' she said, as if she'd been reading my thoughts.

'Great,' I said, 'if we get everyone in the Caribbean to understand the problem, then perhaps we can eventually find a way to educate every other nation in the world, too.'

CHAPTER THIRTY-SIX
New Divers

'With your Mum getting involved in the discussion with the Mayor about the problems with trawling, she'll need to understand the damage being done to the sea bed by the bad trawling methods,' Dan said.

Tom and I were sat with Dan at breakfast.

'You can already swim, can't you Tom?' asked Dan, 'so, as soon as Sarah's comfortable with swimming, then I'll teach you both to dive, then I can show you what we're talking about.'

Dan had promised to teach Mum to swim as her birthday present from him and he'd devoted time for individual lessons for her over the past few weeks. She showed herself to be a quick learner and there had been no sign of any nervousness from her about going in the water.

'Dan's such a good teacher,' said Mum. 'I hope I don't let him down on my first dive, but he's insisting I'll be okay. He's put it in the diary for next Saturday. It's great that Tom's going to be learning to dive too.'

'You'll be fine, Mum,' I said. 'Dan wouldn't be taking you both down if he thought you weren't ready. He worries all the time about safety, so if he says you're ready to dive in the ocean, then you'll be fine.'

I remembered how much I'd enjoyed my first dive over the coral reef. 'You're going to love it, Mum.'

Dan asked Jack, and Sol to come out with us on Mum and Tom's first dive, and suggested we go out to the sandy plain just past Rocky Reef.

'That'll be a good place,' said Sol, 'if we go out there, then both Tom and your Mum will see for themselves the sort of creatures living in the sand and which sea bed animals the trawlers are destroying.'

Our plan was hatched!

Saturday dawned sunny and bright, as it always did on our amazing Caribbean island. Once again, I took up my usual position in the water as Mum and Tom got ready to enter, ready to help them if they got into difficulties. Tom did a perfect long stride entry, quickly followed by Mum and soon Dan, Mum, Tom, Jack and I were underwater and heading downwards towards the sandy plain, levelling off at about eighteen metres below the surface. Sol, once again was happy to be boat captain and stayed with the boat, watching our safety buoy and ready to move closer when we were ready to surface.

The previous day must have had a sea swell, as the sand on the sea bed was patterned by ripples of water movement. Swell moves the sand gently from side to side, but I was pleased this was one day when the swell was very gentle. I'd suffered from the constant movement of a big swell in the past and it had a strange effect on me, constantly pushing me forwards, then dragging me back again so I ended up feeling quite sea sick. But not today. The sea was behaving itself and showing off all its beauty.

The seabed ahead of us was gently sloping downwards. The soft sand, a yellow-white colour, had soft corals, and hard fan corals settled into it. Dan got so close to the sea bed I thought his fins would blow up clouds of small sand particles but he was an experienced diver and could get his face close to the sand to look for creatures, yet bend his legs upwards from the back of his knees so his fins were away from the sand. He looked just like an astronaut moving around in a space capsule, as he could turn and twist his body, even go upside down, in the similar weightless environment of the underwater world.

He made a signal for us to form a search pattern, so we spread out, just a metre apart but in a line across the seabed. Mum stayed at one end, as she kept touching the sand with her fins. When she created a sand cloud at the end of the line it didn't disturb the rest of us, and we could still see around our own patch where we were searching.

Dan had a small steel rod which he banged against his dive tank when he wanted our attention.

I heard the banging and I looked towards him. Dan was waving, wanting us to go towards him. We all gathered around him as he pointed at the sea bed. At first, I could see nothing but sand.

Dan gently disturbed the sand with his fingers, and in front of his hand, the sand suddenly moved … a blue-spotted ray raised itself up from underneath the sand where it was hiding and swam through the water away from us. The flat, heart-shaped body had a long, thin tail at the rear, which contained a small sting, but this ray was not like the giant stingrays whose stings could really hurt us ... this was just a little ray which preferred to swim away from us rather than turn to sting us. It moved skillfully through the water with undulating movements of its body. The blue spots across its back were beautiful, and the sides of its body were shaped into flowing wing-like structures. The ray looked like it was flying through the water as it moved. Mum's eyes seemed to get bigger behind her mask as she watched this amazing sea creature at twenty metres below the surface of the ocean.

CHAPTER THIRTY-SEVEN
Creatures in the Sand

We'd all spread out in our search pattern again and had been looking for only another few moments, when I heard Dan tapping on his dive tank once more with his steel rod. This time he was pointing forward.

Ahead of us was a shoal of garden eels, sticking their thin, worm-like little bodies out of the sand and looking around. They were as small as our fingers, wriggling and watching out for danger, whilst trying to catch small particles of food in the water.

As we got closer, they gradually disappeared back into the sand. The eels closest to us slipped beneath the sand first, then as we moved towards them, the rest of the eels all disappeared. We swam over their homes in the sand. I turned and watched where they had been, and it took only a few seconds after we'd passed over them, before they started to pop up again to look around and feed.

Dan also pointed out a small goby fish, which looked like it was standing on the sand. It had two tough fins acting like stubby legs and it used its tail to balance itself. Beside it was a little shrimp which was constantly pushing sand out of a hole. It looked like the fish was standing guard whilst the shrimp worked … then as we got closer, both the shrimp and the little fish both hurriedly disappeared down the hole which the shrimp had been making.

Then more of my favourites … some yellow-headed

jawfish. In the sand they did the same thing as the sand eels and slid downwards with their tails going into the sand, but they made a much bigger hole than the sand eels and they popped up and down like tiny jack-in-a-box toys connected to a metal spring.

A snake eel was hiding near the reef with just its pale-spotty-coloured head sticking out of the sand, but I knew its body was well hidden, and behind its head could be a body and tail of over a metre or more in length, all buried in the sand. Although called a snake eel because it was long and thin, it wasn't dangerous like sea snakes in other parts of the world and could never bite or hurt us.

A flat fish … a peacock flounder suddenly moved in front of us. It had been totally camouflaged on the sand, then as it moved, it gave me a bit of a fright, although once I realised what it was, I relaxed, knowing it was harmless.

Tom, as a novice diver, was the first to run low on air so we all surfaced with him and returned to the boat.

'That was amazing,' said Mum. 'I couldn't believe how many different creatures were living in the sand.'

'It was incredible,' Tom agreed, nodding his head.

The two of them couldn't stop talking about the animals they'd seen. 'I can't believe there are so many strange, but beautiful creatures down there,' said Mum.

'Yep,' said Tom, 'that really was a great experience.'

'Out of all the things we've just seen,' said Dan, 'it's only the flounders that humans eat. All the other creatures we saw just live their lives happily without any interruptions from humans, unless of course, fishermen use trawling equipment. When that happens, the trawler's machinery moves across the sand and picks up everything that lives there. By the time the fishermen empty the net into their boat, and the flounder fish are put to one side to be taken to the fish market, all the other creatures we've seen today are dead. They'd be thrown back into the water, having been killed for no purpose at all. It's such a waste of life.'

'That's so terrible,' said Mum.

Tom was nodding in agreement. 'I can't comprehend why the fishermen don't understand for themselves, when they see all the dead animals that they've killed.'

'So many different species are being killed unnecessarily by trawling,' said Dan, 'it's really not good for the diversity of life in the ocean. The ocean has hundreds of different animals ... animals we don't see on land ... yet they get killed before we even understand what's down there.'

Mum was shocked. She'd particularly liked the yellow-headed jawfish.

'Those jawfish looked like they were dancing,' she said, 'and the little shrimp and goby fish which lived together with the fish standing guard whilst the shrimp kept their hidey-hole ready. I really loved the way they were working together to keep safe. If trawling means these creatures are being destroyed for no good reason at all, then I can promise you all, I'm going to do everything I can to stop trawling around these beautiful underwater areas.'

'Yes,' I agreed. 'We have to fight to save these creatures … nobody else seems to care.'

CHAPTER THIRTY-EIGHT
We Need a Boat!

With Tom heading back to California to arrange the purchase of a Fisheries Protection Boat, Sol, Jack and I seemed to have nothing to do. We were still banned from using the RIB, so on Sunday we started our day early, with a beach clean-up. We were putting the sacks containing our collection of plastics and other rubbish by Joel's hut behind Drifters, when Joel turned up for his day's work.

'I know we're banned from using the RIB,' I said to Joel, 'but I'd like to get back to Pirates' Peak beach and check out what was inside those boxes in the cave.'

'Yeah, me too,' said Jack. 'I'd love to go back there. It might be pirates' treasure!'

'I asked my Dad if we could borrow one of the hire boats,' said Sol, 'but he said that Dan was right and we shouldn't be allowed to use any of the boats for a while. After hearing we'd got trapped, he and my Mum are worrying about us too. They've been nagging me every day since about how stupid we were not to tell anyone what we were planning to do.'

'Yeah, the same with my Mum and Dad,' said Jack. 'They reckon I was lying to Uncle Dan, so I've been in the 'dog-house' for a while too.'

'Well, there might be an answer,' said Joel, 'if you young 'uns are looking for some'at to do? You needs a boat eh? Well if you looks behind all them broken beach chairs in the hut, yous might find some'at which you could do a bit o' mending of. Be good for yous to learn how to get it all back together again.'

'What are you talking about, Joel?' I asked. 'What are you suggesting we mend?'

'Well, you take a look, young lady, and you might just find an old sailing dinghy in the back of that hut. It's been there a while now and needs a bit o' work, but I reckons you three could get it all set for going to sea, again.'

Jack rushed into the hut. 'Where? Where is it, Joel? It sounds perfect. We can mend it, can't we and then we can sail over to Pirates' Peak again and check out the cave and the treasure?'

The old hut that Joel used for storing all the beach chairs and umbrellas was much more than a normal hut. It was the size of a barn. There was so much rubbish in the back we couldn't immediately find what we were looking for. When we found it, we pulled it out onto the beach. The old sailing dinghy was about five metres long by two metres wide.

'This is great,' said Sol, 'we could all get in this and sail it over to go and see our cave.'

It had a couple of holes in the hull and there were no sails to be found, but that didn't deter us from deciding we had a project to work on.

'We could get bits of wood to glue over those holes,' said Sol. 'That'd be easy.'

'What about sails though,' I said. 'Doesn't a sailing dinghy need sails?'

'Yeah, well, Dad's got loads of old stuff from the hire boats,' said Sol, 'I'm sure we can get hold of something.'

'You get them holes fixed up,' said Joel, 'then you cans use it, but you kids'll have to tell us grown-ups what yous planning to do and where yous going. We don't want no more of them adventures of you three getting trapped in a cave, again. No, you kids have gotta be up front and honest with us about what yous gonna do.'

CHAPTER THIRTY-NINE
Dinghy Repairs

I remembered my first impressions of Pontus Island all those months ago. As Mum and I had been driven across the island from the airport to Jude's Bay, everywhere I looked seemed untidy. There were piles of rubble in almost every garden.

'Hurricanes,' the taxi driver had told us. 'Hurricane damage causes problems every few years and islanders keep everything that gets blown down, to help with repairs in the future.'

It looked like nobody ever threw anything away. But, today, that was useful to us.

After Jack and Sol had worked out what we needed, Sol and I went on a fantastic trip around the area to collect all sorts of spare parts for our dinghy project. Between us we begged our families, neighbours, even businesses for permission to look around the yards and gardens for what we needed.

We spent the whole day working on the dinghy. I was amazed how we were able to source a saw, wood, and glue to repair the woodwork and a screwdriver to check all the fittings.

Jack borrowed some tools from his Dad's garage and it wasn't long before we were sawing and hammering bits of wood into the right size and shape for the repairs that were needed. We worked on our sailboat project for the rest of the day.

After school on Monday we decided our boat was fit enough to try out in the water.

We launched it off the beach and I was tasked with holding the rope to stop it floating away whilst Jack and Sol went over the whole boat looking for leaks or areas that still needed repair. But it was fine. We had a seaworthy boat and now we needed sails.

The three of us wandered across to Byron's Boat Hire area at the end of Dolphin Beach. Sol asked his Dad if there were any spare sails we could borrow.

'You can take a look,' said Byron, 'but I think that pile of old sails are pretty hopeless. They've nearly all got holes and tears in them. That's why they's discarded over there.

'We began to sort out the sails and it was surprisingly heavy work. Sails on dinghies look so tiny when you look at them sailing from off the beach, but when you got close up, I realised they were very large, and each sail was heavy. We searched through the pile for a while but all we saw were sails which had big holes and rips in.

'No way are we mending these,' said Jack, as he walked further around the big pile of canvas.

Then he stopped and was looking through a pile of metal objects.

'What about an old engine?' he said.

'What sort of engine?' Sol asked.

'Here, look,' said Jack, 'there's half a dozen old outboard motors here. Aren't they used anymore?'

'No, I don't think so,' said Sol. 'I think Dad's put them here cos he can't get the motors started anymore.'

'Umm,' said Jack.

'What are you thinking, Jack?' I asked.

'I'm thinking,' he said smiling, 'I'm thinking ... that my Dad runs a garage and I've learnt a lot from him about motors. If we carry one of these over to Dad's garage, I'll see if I can fix it. Dad'll be pleased to see me messing about with an engine, he's always saying I spend too much time on my bodyboard in the sea.'

'I'll find out if we can have one,' said Sol. He wandered off to see his Dad, and I could see Bryon nodding. Sol ran back.

'Yep, we can take any of these and see if we can get one going,' he said.

'Right,' I said, 'let's move to Plan B and turn our sailing dinghy into a small motorboat, then we can get across to Pirates' Peak beach.'

Sol and Jack took one end each of an outboard engine and carried it across to 'Pete's Garage'.

Sol and I left Jack to work on the engine, whilst we designed an extra-strong piece of wood to be added to the stern to help hold the engine on tight. We also designed and fitted a cover for the centre board hole.

'A sailing boat has a centre board,' explained Sol. 'It's a moveable piece of wood that goes through the centre of the boat and sticks out beneath it to stop the dinghy being swept sideways in the water when the sails are up. But seeing as we're not using sails now, we don't need the centre board. We can just block up the hole and then our sailing dinghy becomes a motor boat.'

Sol and I finished our tasks quite quickly, then sat planning what we needed to take with us once we had a fully working boat.

'It'll have to be next weekend now,' said Sol.

'Hopefully,' I said, 'but Jack's got to work some magic on that engine first.'

We listed some of the things we'd taken with us before. Ropes, torches, first aid kit, water and food.

'Just in case!' I said.

'We ought to have a way of contacting someone,' said Sol.

'We could take Mum's phone with us,' I suggested. 'She'd be happier if she thought we could phone someone if we got into trouble.'

'The only problem with that is the phone signals aren't too good once we're away from the main towns on the island,' said Sol.

Jack could hear us talking.

'I've got an old walkie-talkie radio set in my bedroom,' he

called out. 'It was a present a few years back. I expect it'll need a couple of new batteries, but I can probably get those from Dad. We could have one walkie-talkie set on the boat and leave the other one with one of the adults.'

'We should give it to Ellen,' I suggested, 'she lives nearest to where we're going, so she should be able to pick up our signal.'

Our plan to return to Pirates' Peak beach and to our cave was taking shape.

CHAPTER FORTY
Back to the Cave

The weekend brought calm winds and as our dinghy motored from Jude's Bay around to Pirates' Peak beach it made its way across a gentle sea with no large waves breaking across the bow.

'Crikey,' said Sol, as he took the tiller. 'This is so slow compared to the RIB.'

'At least we've got ourselves some transport,' I said, 'It makes a change not to be getting wet though.'

Our small boat gave us a gentle ride. Nothing like riding in the RIB at full speed with the bow lifting off the water and crashing down on the surface, creating enormous splashes. The small outboard engine gave out a putt-putt sound at the stern as it pushed our little boat forward. It made its way through the water smoothly with the movement almost luring you into a soothing, dreamlike state. It was so relaxing.

We'd already made sure that everyone knew where we were going.

'Why do you need to go back to the cave?' asked Dan

'We never found out what was in those packages, did we?' I said. 'If we can get into the cave by moving some small rocks from the entrance then we might be able to see what's stored there.'

'Well, you go carefully,' warned Dan, 'check that walkie-talkie set works before you go inside.'

'This trip's taking us ages.' Sol moaned again.

He was obviously missing the thrill of travelling at speed across the water.

'At last,' he said, as we eventually approached the beach.

Pulling our little boat across the sand was easy, and we soon had it hidden by leaves under the trees.

We took out the rucksacks. This time we had included the walkie-talkie system that Jack had found under his bed.

'We can test it now, to see if Ellen can hear us.' he said.

'Jack calling Ellen, Jack calling Ellen,' he spoke into the handset.

The handset crackled a bit, then we heard Ellen's voice.

'Where are you?' she asked.

'We've just arrived on Pirates' Peak beach,' said Jack. 'We're gonna walk up towards the cave now.'

'Okay then. Go carefully,' said Ellen, 'I'll keep a listen out for you.'

'Will the walkie-talkies work inside the cave?' I asked Jack.

'Um! Not sure,' said Jack, 'we'll have to try them out when we get inside.'

'Come on,' I said, 'let's get up there and see if we can move some stones from the entrance.'

We walked along the beach until we found our pirates' path, then headed up straight up through the rainforest.

'I don't remember a stream here last time,' said Sol. 'It must have been dried up, but look now, just by the path, there's a stream of water rushing down the side of the mountain.'

'Probably coming from the waterfall,' I said, 'the water's moving very fast.'

'I wonder if any of the smugglers have been here since we last came,' said Sol, as we climbed the hill up to the cave entrance.

'Hey, look ... the cave's open,' shouted Jack.

'Sshh, Jack,' I whispered, 'we don't know if there's anyone in there now, do we? Let's stay quiet and just creep up close.'

We could see the rocks had been moved away from the entrance leaving a fairly small gap.

Jack began to climb up the rocks outside.

'Go slowly,' whispered Sol.

'Then stop and listen,' I said quietly.

'Yeah, okay,' Jack whispered. 'I'll go and see if anyone's there.'

Sol and I watched Jack's progress. He got close to the entrance, then stopped for a few minutes, listening.

Then he slowly entered the cave.

It seemed ages before his head appeared back at the entrance gap

'It's okay,' he called out. 'There's nobody home. But it looks like an extra load of parcels have been delivered.'

Sol and I quickly joined Jack in the cave.

'Crikey, look at all that!' said Sol. He was looking at a pile of parcels, all well taped up with a waterproof covering. 'There's easily twice the amount compared to the last time we were here.'

CHAPTER FORTY-ONE
Smugglers

'What's that noise?' I asked. I could hear a buzzing sound.

Sol went to the cave entrance and looked out. 'It's a boat coming this way,' he said. 'Looks like it's heading for the beach below us. I don't think we got time to get back down to our boat, or even into the rainforest,' said Sol. 'They're coming in fast now. Crikey, they're in a hurry, they're on the beach already.'

'Okay,' I said, 'let's get to the back of the cave, perhaps go down the tunnel out of sight. We don't want to be seen, but I'd like to be close enough to hear what they're talking about.'

'Right,' said Jack, 'check you've got everything. We don't want to show them that anyone else's been in here.'

We slipped into the first tunnel area and settled ourselves behind some large rocks.

It was only moments before they arrived. Puffing and looking hot, three men came into the cave. All three of them were carrying more parcels.

We listened to their plans. 'That's it, pile 'em up over there with the other stuff,' said one voice. 'There's one more load to bring over. We can do that tomorrow. Then that's the last load from Mexico.'

'Okay, Harry,' said another voice. 'Then, I'll contact the Florida gang to come and collect it all. They'll get down here pretty quick, I expect.'

'I don't like the fact that we left the entrance open last time,' said another voice. 'We need to ensure no one can find all this.'

'Yeah, it's too valuable to lose,' said the voice I thought was Harry. 'We'll close up after we leave.'

Just then, the walkie talkie in Jack's rucksack started to crackle. Ellen must've been trying to talk to us, but the signal was bad inside the cave. Jack reached in and switched it off fast but the smugglers had heard a noise.

I made signs to the others and we silently moved further back and separated out.

'I'm sure I heard something back here.'

The smuggler called Harry was heading our way to investigate the sound.

I peeked out from behind my big rock. Harry was tall, untidily dressed and unshaven. He was looking around but didn't seem to have seen us.

'Nah, must've been a bat or som'at stretching its wings and flapping while it's asleep probably. Yeah, just an animal noise. There's nothing here.'

I tried to move carefully, but my feet slipped away from under my body and I found myself splatting down on a wet section of the cave floor. I put my hand out to try to keep myself still and not make a noise. My hand stopped me from falling but it hit something hard and somehow, I knew it wasn't a rock. I looked down and saw a small box made of wood with carving along the top. I quickly picked it up and slipped it into my rucksack. I'll look at it later, I thought.

I turned back to see the smugglers exiting through the hole where we had all entered.

Then I heard an awful noise. They were shifting rocks to close the hole up again. I couldn't believe it. Within minutes the hole was closed again from the outside.

The cave had gone dark. Once again, we were trapped inside.

CHAPTER FORTY-TWO

Parcels

'Well, at least we know the way out now,' said Jack, as he bent to reach inside his rucksack for his torch. 'Should be easy as pie this time. Then when we get to the side of the well, we can use the walkie-talkie to contact Ellen.'

'Yes,' said Sol, 'she should be able to get a signal that close.'

'Ellen will just have to rescue us again,' said Sol. 'But she seemed to enjoy it last time, and now she's remembered how to use the remote-control winch, it shouldn't be too difficult for her.'

'Before we set off though, can we take a look at these parcels,' I said. 'We know the way out now and won't need to save our torch batteries quite so much this time. Let's use some of our torchlight to find out what's in the boxes.'

Jack opened the nearest box. He reached inside and took out the top parcel. He carefully unwrapped it whilst Sol and I held our torches so we could all see what he was doing.

'It's tightly packaged, with lots of tape and protective bubble stuff around it,' he commentated.

I could see him pulling at a top corner, and the wrapping was becoming loose.

He began to pull out a large object.

'It's very heavy,' said Jack.

My torch began to glint on the item as it was unwrapped.

'Wow!' said Jack. 'This looks like something made of gold.'

He pulled away more of the wrapping and soon held the complete object in his hand.

It was a dagger. A gold dagger!

'Careful, Jack, don't cut yourself,' I warned.

He laid the dagger on the ground and started on another parcel.

This time he unwrapped what looked like a block of carved rock. 'It's so heavy,' said Jack.

As he turned it round in his hand, I yelled out.

'It's a snake head ... look, it's some sort of carving of the head of a one of those poisonous snakes.'

'Yeah, it looks like a cobra head,' said Sol.

'But look at the colour,' said Jack. 'This is gold too.'

I could not believe what we were seeing.

'This is treasure,' said Jack, 'but it's not pirates who put it here.'

'I reckon these men are part of a gang of thieves who've stolen stuff. This looks like the sort of things you seen in museums,' I said. 'Artefacts ... that's the word. These parcels contain stolen artefacts! Those men talked about it coming from Mexico. Perhaps they've stolen it all from sites of historic interest, like old tombs or something like that.'

'Yeah,' said Jack, 'I've read about the tomb of Tutankhamun in Egypt. That tomb held all sort of treasures, but these men were talking about Mexico.'

'It could be from an ancient Mayan civilisation,' I said. 'If so, this stuff is incredibly valuable.'

'Come on, let's get going,' said Sol. 'We need to get back and tell the police and customs what's going on. They'll have to get over here tomorrow and catch these men when they make their final delivery.'

Jack carefully wrapped the dagger and the snake head carving, then placed them into his rucksack. 'If I take these with us, then the police will believe our story.'

'We can't leave them here unwrapped anyway,' I said, 'or the smugglers will know someone's been here.'

'Come on,' said Sol. He was obviously anxious to find our way out of the cave again.

We all had torches, and could see ahead quite well, but the rocks were wetter than previously.

'That stream outside was flowing fast, wasn't it?' I said, 'perhaps the water from the waterfall is finding its way into the cave system too?'

As we headed along the tunnel, I heard Sol yell out and turned back to find him.

'I've just slipped on that wet rock,' said Sol, 'I think I've twisted my ankle. I'm not sure I can walk.'

CHAPTER FORTY-THREE
Lost

Jack came back to find us. 'I think I put a bandana in my rucksack,' he said. 'We could use that as a bandage to stop your ankle from wobbling around so much. Sit down, Sol, let's get you sorted. Doing this should support your ankle and you should be able to hobble along. Here, Lucy … you're better at these things. Can you get this round Sol's ankle?'

I worked with the bandana, wrapping it around Sol's ankle and tying it so it would stay on. Sol now had some support around his foot.

'Right now, we've dealt with Sol's problem, let's get out of here,' said Jack.

What Jack didn't realise as he walked off, was between stopping and starting off again, he'd changed direction and was no longer walking on our known route of escape. He'd mistakenly turned at an angle and was going down a different tunnel to the side of us.

Neither Sol nor I noticed either, as we followed Jack, with me helping Sol to his feet and getting him used to walking with a painful ankle.

We had walked for some distance before I realised something was wrong.

'Hang on, Jack,' I called, 'are we going in the right direction? I don't remember our previous way out having any downhill sections ... and this slope is definitely going down fairly steeply.'

'You're right,' said Jack, 'I was wondering the same thing, but there's something ahead of us. Let's investigate that first.'

We emerged from our downhill tunnel into a large cave and saw an enormous lake of water ahead of us.

'Hang on,' said Jack. 'You know where we are, don't you?'

'Where?' asked Sol.

'This is the cave where we surfaced, isn't it?' said Jack. 'When we dived down to the black hole at the edge of the reef ... this is where we came up and talked and put our torches out to see the darkness.'

'Well,' I said, 'it's good that we found the link back to the original underwater cave entrance but this isn't going to help us find the right way out is it? We can't escape from the caves down through the water, can we? We've got no diving gear ... and now we've lost our original exit back to Ellen's house.

'Yep,' said Jack, 'I think we've got ourselves properly lost this time.'

CHAPTER FORTY-FOUR
Skeletons in the Cave?

I began to imagine three skeletons being found in the caves in the future. Would we ever find our way out? I decided to keep my thoughts to myself.

'The water seems to be trickling down,' said Sol, 'I can hear it. Looks like water is seeping down here quite quickly.'

'We need to find our way out of here before we get stopped by water filling up the tunnels and flooding the whole system,' I said.

'Come on, let's go back up,' said Sol. 'We can't get out through here.'

'I remember feeling fresh air the first time we came here,' said Jack. He stood still then turn slowly in a circle.

'Yep ... that's it! That way!' he was pointing to the left. 'That's where the fresh air is coming from.'

He moved quickly towards the left-hand side of the cave.

'I think we need to squeeze through here,' said Jack, indicating a pile of rocks, 'then go through this next tunnel.'

We all squeezed through.

'That's it,' I said, 'now the tunnel is going back up again, so we're going away from sea level.'

I looked back and could see that Sol was struggling. He was obviously in pain from his ankle.

'Come on, Sol, keep going.' I tried to encourage him.

There was no way I was going to leave him in the cave and go find help without him. There were so many different routes through the caves we might never find him again.

Whenever I could, I supported him with his arm around my shoulder, but it was often too narrow for more than one person at a time, as we squeezed through holes between the different parts of the cave system.

'Nearly there,' said Jack, 'that smells like the rain forest air ahead of us.'

He was right, within another five minutes we had found an exit. This time we came out in the rainforest, way below Ellen's house.

'Looks like no-one's been in or out of here for years,' said Jack. 'There isn't even a path. Come on, it's machete time again.'

Jack and I cut a thin pathway through the forest, heading down to the beach. Sol rested his ankle and waited for us to cut through the heavy foliage.

'I love these creeper things attached to the trees,' said Jack. 'Hey look, you can swing on them just like in those jungle stories. Jack couldn't resist reaching up and suspending himself from the tendrils that hung down from the trees. He was soon looking like a monkey, dangling and spinning around.

'Come on, Jack,' said Sol, 'we need to tell the police what the smugglers said about coming back tomorrow.'

'Yeah, okay, give me a break,' said Jack. 'It's hard work

cutting all this stuff down with my machete while you just sit there!'

Sol looked a bit sad. I knew he'd be wanting to help but knew he couldn't manage it.

'Hey, Sol,' I said, 'can you get the walkie-talkie out of Jack's rucksack and get in touch with Ellen? Tell her what's happened and she can contact the police whilst we get ourselves out of here.'

'Great idea, Lucy,' said Sol. 'I can do that sitting down.'

It was another hour before we had a pathway back to the beach.

Jack and I pulled the dinghy down to the water and helped Sol get into the small boat.

Sol immediately sat next to the tiller. A big smile on his face.

'Now, this I can do without standing up,' he said.

Jack started the engine and Sol moved the tiller to navigate our dinghy away from the beach and we headed for Jude's Bay and the jetty leading to the Dive Centre.

Ellen had arranged for Dan to meet us and help Sol get some medical attention.

As I told Dan what had happened, he shook his head and sighed.

'You've got away with it again,' he said. 'You must be using magic spells to get you out of all this trouble.'

'Well, at least we didn't end up as skeletons, did we?' I said.

'Not this time,' said Dan, 'but you've certainly been using up your quota of luck over these past few weeks.'

'I think we found the back door to the cave, Uncle Dan,' said Jack. 'It's much easier than clambering out of Ellen's well.'

'Trouble is,' said Sol, 'I'm not sure of the route we took through the tunnels to get out this time. If we ever get stuck again, I still don't think I'd know our way out.'

'Well, that's not a problem is it?' I said.

The others both looked at me with crossed eyebrows.

'What d'you mean, Lucy?' asked Sol.

'Well,' I said, 'you don't honestly think I'm daft enough to get trapped in that cave ever again, do you?'

CHAPTER FORTY-FIVE
Police and Customs

The police and customs men came to interview us all that evening and took the information they needed. We handed over our treasure trove, but not before Mum had sneakily taken some photos of the two items we had taken from the cave.

'I'm going to do some research and see if I can find where these items have come from,' she said. 'I get the feeling I've seen a picture of this dagger somewhere before.'

'Can we ask you to take us out in your Dive Boat early tomorrow morning, please?' The policeman in charge, was speaking to Dan.

We'd like you to drop us off on the beach and then move your boat a few hundred yards offshore, to wait for us.'

A local uniformed customs man with a well-clipped, tidy beard introduced himself as Marvin.

'If the smugglers see your boat,' he explained, 'they'll just think you're diving. If we scare them off with our official looking boat, they might not land on the beach. We need to catch them red-handed.'

'We'll need you youngsters to help, too,' said Marvin. 'You'll have to guide us to the path and take us to the cave entrance.'

Marvin turned to Dan. 'It's alright though, we shan't put them in any danger. Once they've taken us to the entrance, then I'll get them to hide in the rainforest area outside.'

Dan nodded. 'I'll tell their parents. As long as you keep them safe, I'm sure they'll agree.'

The following day, Sol's ankle had improved so much, he insisted on joining us.

'Are you sure, Sol?' I asked. 'Aren't you still in pain?'

'Just a little bit,' admitted Sol honestly, 'but it's better than yesterday, and I was able to walk a bit then, wasn't I?' he said. 'You're not leaving me here while you two have all the fun of catching the smugglers.'

He was probably in more pain than he was admitting but I think he would have said anything not to be left behind.

One policeman was assigned to accompany Sol who was to take him into the rainforest.

'I'll take him up to the exit we used yesterday,' said Sol. 'It'll be just like a television programme. When the police are banging down the front door, the criminals often try to run out of the back of the house. But we'll be waiting at the back entrance of the cave, just in case! We won't let them escape.'

We waved Sol and his new policeman friend off, as they headed up the new path to the cave exit.

Meanwhile, the rest of us headed for the path up to the main cave entrance.

Jack and I were allowed to guide Marvin and Nick, the customs men, to the cave where we found the treasure.

We walked up, along the pirates' path, accompanied by

two extra policemen, then took them inside the cave and showed them the big boxes of wrapped treasure, then the area at the back of the cave, where we'd hidden previously.

'Now, you need to leave us in here,' said Marvin. 'Our two policemen can put the rocks back across the entrance. We don't want to leave the entrance open and warn the smugglers that anyone's inside.'

'You've done a grand job so far, Lucy,' said Marvin, 'But there's no way we're going to let you and Jack stay in the cave. It's far too dangerous. You need to be outside and safe.'

'We want you youngsters to hide in the rainforest,' said Nick. 'The policemen who close up the cave can stay nearer the cave but will also stay hidden in the forest area.'

We wandered back down the path towards the beach. Once we'd decided where to hide, we both sat with our backs against trees, well out of sight of the path.

'We should be able to hear anyone who is tramping up from the beach,' said Jack.

It wasn't long before we heard an engine.

The sound of the boat engine came closer.

We sat as still as was possible. I listened to the beat of my heart getting faster. I wondered if anyone else could hear it.

Puffing and wheezing, the three men we'd heard in the cave came stumbling past us carrying their load of parcels. They climbed the path, too out of breath to talk. We counted as they passed.

One, two, three.

They were heading for the cave.

When they reached the cave, it must have looked just like they'd left it. There were no clues to the fact that the cave entrance had been opened and shut again, and that now there were two customs men waiting inside for them to incriminate themselves.

I felt it wouldn't be long before the smugglers would be arrested and in handcuffs.

CHAPTER FORTY-SIX
Smuggler on the Run

Jack sat looking up at the trees growing straight above us.

'Hey, Lucy, I think I've got an idea,' he said. 'If we pull hard, some of these creepers might come down.'

'Why do we want to do that?' I asked.

'Well, I've watched police programmes on the television,' said Jack. 'I've seen them use what's called a stinger ... where the police put this metal thing across the road. It's got spikes in it. The robbers or whoever, go storming off in their getaway car and then don't see the stinger ahead of them. They drive right across it ... and of course, the spikes go into the wheels making the tyres go flat, so the car won't go any further and the police arrest them.'

'So, what's that got to do with the tree creepers,' I asked.

'Easy,' said Jack. 'The creepers can act as our stingers. If we stretch one across the path every few metres and we sit hidden either side of the path holding the creeper, then if the smugglers are running down the path, we can pull on a creeper ... it'll go up in the air and we'll trip the smugglers up.'

'Hey, that's not a bad idea, Jack.'

'Come on then, let's get organised ... there's no time to waste.'

We pulled at the nearest creeper and with both of us putting all our weight on it, we managed to pull it down to the ground.

We dragged the creeper out of the forest and across the path. Jack helped me to pull it almost straight then wriggled it a bit to make it look like it had fallen naturally.

'I think we can only have one creeper for this idea, Jack,' I said. 'I can't see how we could get to a different one quickly enough ... I think just one will have to do.'

'Okay, you stay this side and I'll go back over to where we were. Let's keep a listen out for anyone coming back from the cave and if we do hear them then we need to time it just right, and both pull together.'

'It would be perfect,' I said, 'if we got the creeper tangled around a smuggler's legs and they fell over ... giving us enough time to tie them up.'

Then I had another idea.

'Actually,' I said, 'we need some more creepers going across the path, in case we need stuff handy, to tie around their legs or something.'

We pulled some more creepers down and laid them across the path. 'Now make sure we both sit by the same creeper,' I said. 'It won't work if we're pulling on two different ones.' I couldn't stop giggling at the thought of us pulling on different creepers and the smugglers getting away.

'Okay, let's try it out,' said Jack.

We pulled our first creeper from either side and whoosh ... it flew up into the air. We practised for a while, until we felt we could do at the right speed.

'Now, let's watch out for a smuggler running down the path,' I said.

It was only minutes before I heard shouting. One of the three smugglers had emerged from the cave and the policeman outside the cave received an enormous punch in the face and landed on his back. Now, there was a smuggler running down the path towards us.

'Get ready,' yelled Jack.

'Now!' he called, and we both pulled on our creeper at the same time.

We had timed it perfectly!

We'd pulled the creeper at exactly the right moment and the creeper had caught around the smuggler's legs. We now had a smuggler laid flat out on the path in front of us. He'd landed awkwardly and his breath had been pushed out of his body as he had fallen. He was totally winded.

'Quick,' yelled Jack, 'let's get him tied up.'

We both ran onto the path and gathered up some of the other creeper foliage.

Jack sat on the smugglers back, stopping him from getting up whilst I tied the smuggler's legs together. I tied one piece of creeper around his ankles. I reached for another tendril and Jack and I worked together to tie the smuggler's hands behind his back.

Within a minute we had him all bound up and unable to

go anywhere. Jack remained sitting on his back though, just to make sure.

At that point the policeman who'd been outside the cave had recovered from the punch he'd received and came running down the path.

'I can't believe it,' he said, 'look what you two have done. That's fantastic, kids. Well done. Come on, let me get these handcuffs on him.'

'This means we've caught them all,' said the policeman, Marvin and Rick have got one man in the cave, and my colleague outside the cave has got another one ... and thanks to you two, we've got the third man, too.'

CHAPTER FORTY-SEVEN
History

A week later Dan came down to Drifters with some good news.

'I heard today there's been a second raid on the caves on Pirates' Peak and the customs men have successfully caught the smugglers who planned to collect the treasure and take it to the United States.'

'Ah! That's the sorta news we like to hear,' said Joel.

'So, they caught everyone,' said Dan. 'Firstly, the smugglers who were delivering the treasure to the cave …'

'Helped by us, of course,' interrupted Jack.

'Yes, Jack, helped by you,' agreed Dan. 'But now they've also caught the ones who would have taken the treasure off to be sold. It means that everyone involved in the whole smuggler ring has now been arrested.'

'Umph! Why didn't they ask us to go with them to help arrest the men who came from Florida?' moaned Jack.

'No, it's alright, Jack,' said Dan, 'they managed to arrest the smugglers without your help this time.'

'Yeah? Only cos we showed 'em how to do it properly, in the first place,' Jack muttered.

'Have we heard yet? What sort of treasure do the experts think it was?' I asked. 'It looked very old to me, and I'd really like to know where it's come from.'

'I took a picture of the dagger and the snake head carving,' said Mum. I've tried to research them but haven't found anything yet. Somehow though, that dagger looks familiar, but I can't think where I might have seen it before.'

'Let's hope someone tells us about it all soon,' said Ellen.

'I've got some news too,' I said. 'A few days ago, I emptied my rucksack properly and found the wooden box I'd recovered from the cave. I can't believe I'd forgotten about it for so long.'

'Is it treasure?' asked Sol.

'Well, I tried to open it, and couldn't, so Mum and I took it to Mrs. Slater at the local history club, to see if she thought it was important.'

'When Mrs. Slater saw the box, she got very excited,' said Mum.

'Yes, she opened it carefully and we found old coins and some jewellery inside,' I said. 'After a quick glance she decided the coins looked like Spanish coins, and they were very old. So, it's possible the box once belonged to a pirate. She's going to research the jewellery next.'

'That's not all,' said Mum, 'Lucy's thrilled about her pirate find,' said Mum, 'but I've found something too.'

'Really!' said Jack, 'what have you got?'

'When we were diving the other day, I collected some plastic rubbish from the seabed, and in amongst it I also found a piece of leather. I thought it was shaped quite oddly, and Mrs. Slater did some research. She phoned me this morning and told me she'd identified it as a piece of ancient history too ... it's a part of a shoe, which could be as old as pirate times too. It seems pirates were in the Caribbean from the 1500s to 1830's. She certainly said it was very old and has been preserved in the sand. She's hoping to find a way of displaying our finds in the little museum at the back of the Library.'

'That's really great,' said Joel, nodding his head.

'Trouble is,' I said, 'there's no money from the Council to pay wages for someone to work in the museum. All that's happened, is that someone's volunteered to put some shelves up around the small room and people have just given a few things in, and none of those items are labelled. There is no proper display of finds at all. There should be glass covered cases to protect the items from the atmosphere, too.'

'I was wondering if Jack, and Sol would volunteer with me?' I asked. 'We could spend a few hours, perhaps just one day a week after school. We're quite good at research now, using Mum's library computers. I'm sure we'd be able to sort out the museum a bit better than it is now, with labels and some researched information.'

'We could ask everyone on the Island to donate anything interesting they've found,' said Jack. 'There could be all sorts of old treasure just sitting in people's homes.'

'I think we ought to research the local pirate stories, too,' said Sol. 'That would make a good wall display. Perhaps the museum could be opened to the public, with a ticket price that could be saved towards improving the facilities at the museum. Lots of tourists should be interested.'

'Yep, Jack and Sol and I can ensure the museum is made bright and sparkly with lots of information and showing loads of new and different artefacts. Even Jack has got used to researching things now and even started to enjoy it rather than moaning that he isn't snorkelling or body surfing.'

'We can start with me finding those pirates' papers,' said Ellen. 'I know it's all there, somewhere in the house.'

'Perhaps we'll find there's pirate treasure at the bottom of your well, Ellen,' said Jack. 'We'd have to abseil down to find it though.'

'That'd be fun,' I said. 'I hope we can do a treasure hunt down there. We might have to put dive kit on. We've no idea how deep that water is at the bottom, do we?'

CHAPTER FORTY-EIGHT
Explorer

On Thursday morning, Mum found the answer to her dagger identification problem.

'I was taking something to the Mayor, at the Council offices next door to the Library,' she explained.

That evening, we were all sitting around a Drifters' table, listening.

'You'll never believe it,' said Mum, 'I walked up the steps and into the offices. I went to the Reception desk and asked to speak to the mayor for a moment or two, and they asked me to sit down in Reception and wait.'

'And ...?' said Jack, as impatient as ever.

'Then I looked up and there it was. A very large painting on the wall. It was an old portrait of somebody dressed like an old-fashioned explorer.'

None of us interrupted her.

'I went over and read the label at the bottom. It said it was a portrait of a man called Arthur Dalrimple. It said he was an owner of a sugar plantation on Pontus in the 1750s and that was still in the days of pirates, too.'

'Go on,' said Jack, as Mum took a breath.

'I went to back to the Reception desk and asked about the man. One of the ladies told me that Arthur Dalrimple was a famous landowner on Pontus and that he was also an explorer in Mexico all those years ago. It seems he was one of the first people to find some Mayan ruins which explains it all, doesn't it?'

I looked at the faces around the table.

'No, Mum,' I said, 'we've got no idea what you're trying to explain. What was so special about this portrait?'

'Oh, sorry, didn't I say? Well, in the painting, Arthur Dalrimple was holding the dagger. Our dagger. The gold dagger from the cave.'

'He'd been an explorer of the Mayan civilisation in Mexico and obviously brought some of the artefacts he'd found, back here to Pontus.'

'I think your smugglers must have found those items and put them with all the other artefacts they'd smuggled in from Mexico,' said Ellen.

'That's sounds quite likely,' said Dan, nodding.

'But the strangest thing of all,' continued Mum, was that Arthur Dalrimple was also famous for being a pirate when he returned back to Pontus after being an explorer in Mexico.'

'So, he was a pirate too?' said Sol, his eyes getting wider.

'Well, the ladies at the Reception desk were all laughing cos I didn't know about him,' said Mum, 'but it seems he was very famous on this island and he used to take the dagger with him everywhere. And, the story goes ... when he was out one day, he had an accident. He dropped the dagger on his foot when he wasn't wearing shoes, and everyone gave him a new name! You'll never guess what his pirate name was?'

Mum was now laughing.

'No, Mum ... just tell us, please?' I said.

'Captain Four-Toes!' she laughed. 'Can you believe it?'

'What! He cut off one of his toes with the dagger?' asked Jack.

'Well, that's the story, but who can believe all the tales of pirates, eh?' said Joel. 'I've heard of him, course I have, but I don't knows if the story about him cutting off his toe is true or not.'

'But, isn't that fantastic,' said Dan, 'that the dagger you found in the cave has such a wonderful history.'

'Do you think the Mexican government will want the dagger back?' Sol asked, 'after all, it is one of their long-lost treasures.'

'Well, even if they do,' I said, 'there's still that painting on the wall. Captain Four-Toes will always be part of the history of Pontus Island, won't he?'

CHAPTER FORTY-NINE
Summit Meeting

The days and weeks galloped by. The Summit Meeting for all the Caribbean Island Governors and Mayors once seemed a long time in the future, but now was getting very close indeed.

I'd worked hard on my speech. I edited it and checked it and typed it up on the computer so I could have a script in front of me, and not forget anything important.

Tom had arrived back on Pontus with a very smart Patrol Boat and we called into the Mayor's office to tell him the news and show him the photographs.

'Well,' said the Mayor, 'thank you again, Tom. You've done an excellent job for this island by acquiring this beautiful boat.'

Tom told him his plans for the employment and training of the Fisheries Protection Officers.

'It all sounds grand,' said the Mayor. 'Well, done Tom.' The two of them shook hands.

The mayor looked again at the photographs of the Patrol Boat.

'Only one thing missing though,' said the Mayor.

'What's that?' asked Tom.

'The boat doesn't have a name,' the Mayor laughed. 'All boats should have a name. I'll have to think about that.'

The Mayor and I next met when I attended the Summit Meeting.

I had Mum sat at the front with me for support, whilst Ellen, Tom, Joel, Dan, Jack and Sol all sat in a row reserved for guests at the back.

The hall was packed. I daren't turn around. My stomach was churning. It was like the nervousness I'd felt when talking to my school for the first time, all over again.

Then the Mayor stood up and introduced me. I felt myself walking to the podium, in a dreamlike state. My body was walking whilst my ears listened to the gentle clapping. Were all these people thinking I was too young to know anything, too young to be talking to them? Were these adults going to be interested in what I had to say? Would they understand the problems I was going to talk to them about?

I arrived at the podium and turned to face the audience. My lungs drew in a vast amount of air as I saw how many people were there. I carefully placed my script on the lectern and waited for the polite applause to fade away.

'There is a threat to our oceans which could kill ALL marine life,' I began.

I waited for a few seconds and looked around the room.

That statement had certainly got their attention.

CHAPTER FIFTY
Work Together

I held onto the sides of the lectern tightly and continued.

'In the Caribbean Sea, and in other oceans of the world there are ships known as supertrawlers. These boats are destroying both the seabed and devastating the large shoal fishing industry. They use illegal sized nets, and no-one is stopping them. They catch everything in these nets as they pass through the oceans. Everything is killed. Only a small proportion of the catch is used for human food everything else is thrown back into the sea ... DEAD!'

I glanced up. Everyone was attentive.

'They also use equipment which is massive and is dragged along the bottom of the ocean, killing everything on the seabed.'

I stopped again and looked up. Yes, they were definitely listening.

'These boats are destroying all life in the oceans. From the tiniest of creatures on the sea bed to vast shoals of fish in the open waters. Food chains are being destroyed and there is only one outcome ... complete devastation of everything that lives in the sea.'

I stopped again. I looked at them and exchanged eye contact with those in the front row.

'We could be the last generation to eat fish,' I said, purposely.

I could hear the intake of breath around the room and see the looks on the faces of the Governors and Mayors.

I continued with the statistics. The facts and figures of the problem. I held nothing back. I told them everything including how the by-catch included dolphins, turtles and manta rays.

'... harmless, but beautiful creatures which are all threatened by these boats.'

Then I told them how I felt.

'I feel helpless,' I admitted. 'We are all helpless until we decide to do something about it. At the moment, everyone is standing back as these greedy factory ships continue to destroy our oceans. We need to take action! NOW!'

There was a rustle of movement, and whispers.

'These people have no morals, no understanding about protecting life in the oceans ... or else they wouldn't be doing this. Are they doing it just for the money they make ... yes, of course they are! This type of fishing has consequences, and these fishermen are not thinking of the future of life in the oceans. They are just destroying everything.'

I paused for breath.

'But we CAN stop them! If you and your governments on these wonderful islands in the Caribbean take action you can pass laws that you ALL use. You can have Fishery Protection patrols and stop these boats. Here in the Caribbean we can set the standards for nations of the world and stop the work of these supertrawlers before it is too late.'

I took in extra air and launched into my final sentence.

'I urge everyone in this room to work together to stop this terrible industry and save the lives of ocean creatures.'

As I stepped away from the podium, I heard the thunder-like noise of applause and clapping. Everyone was on their feet.

I returned to Mum, who squeezed my hand, tightly.

When the audience had resumed their seats, our Mayor spoke to thank me.

'It is our duty,' he said, 'to listen to the younger generation. To understand the many problems that are being caused around this wonderful planet, and to do everything we can to protect it.'

He looked around the room.

'I will be working with all of you to address the problem of supertrawlers, and I know by working together we can stop their activities and ensure the oceans are protected.'

CHAPTER FIFTY-ONE
Thank You

We stood on a newly built pontoon in Pontus Harbour.

The Mayor had invited us all to attend a naming ceremony for the Patrol Boat which was tied up to the pontoon. It was all shiny and polished, with large tarpaulin covers hiding the new name, over the bow and stern.

There were journalists, photographers and even a television broadcast camera waiting for the naming ceremony. A television presenter was talking to a camera, explaining the need for a Fishery Protection Boat around the coast of Pontus Island.

'I'm dying to know what the Mayor's decided to call the boat,' said Mum.

'We'll soon know,' said Dan.

The adults had a glass of champagne each, and Jack, Sol and I had been given orange juice to toast the new boat.

The Mayor was wearing his chain of office and looking very smart. He was standing next to a small wooden structure which had a swing rope tied to a bottle of champagne.

'It gives me great pleasure,' he said when the cameras were all pointed towards him, 'to name this new Patrol Boat … 'Lady' …'

He stopped with his hand resting on the release button for the champagne bottle. He nodded to the men who were waiting to pull off the tarpaulin covers.

The name was visible. We could all see it.

'I name this ship 'Lady Lucy',' announced the Mayor, 'in honour of Lucy's hard work to protect ocean creatures.'

My eyes were wide, and I couldn't stop smiling. I almost dropped my glass of orange juice.

'Oh, wow! Thank you so much,' I managed to talk at last. 'That's really great, yes, thank you.'

I was hugged by Tom, and Dan and Mum. Then hugged again by Joel, and Ellen.

'Well deserved, young Lucy,' said Joel, 'well deserved.'

'It's not just me though, is it?' I argued. 'Jack, Sol and me … with Tom and the rest of you …we all work together.'

Jack and Sol stood together. Jack was smiling. 'Everyone knows we help, too,' said Jack, 'but it's right to have your name on the boat, Luce, … it's you who leads the way. It's you who stands up and gets the message out, don't you? I could never talk in front of all those people, like you did the other day. It's you who helps so many people understand the problems.'

Sol was nodding too. He squeezed my arm. 'It's great the Mayor understands the importance of what you said the other day to all those Island leaders. Well done, Lucy. When this protection boat goes out to stop any illegal behaviour, then it'll represent all of us.'

'I have one last duty today,' said the Mayor. We all followed him as he strode back closer to the boat repair yard.

'To celebrate today, I have bought a present for Lucy, Jack and Sol. I'd heard you all needed something, so here you are … from me personally as a thank you for everything you three are doing for the ocean life around this island.'

We stood looking at a tarpaulin sheet covering a big lump on the ground.

He pulled it away.

'I have great pleasure,' said the Mayor, 'in presenting the three of you with a set of sails for your little dinghy.'

As the tarpaulin was pulled away, our little boat could be seen, and a set of smart new sails lay alongside it.

'Hey, that's amazing!' said Jack.

'Now we can teach you to sail properly too, Lucy,' said Sol.

'Hang on,' I said. '… look … our boat's got a name too.'

Along the top edge of the bow and on the stern … our dinghy now had gold lettering …

'Ocean Guardians'

'I love it,' I said. 'Thank you so much.' My eyes were starting to feel damp and the hugging started all over again.

****

SCIENCE STUFF
Lucy's Dive Equipment

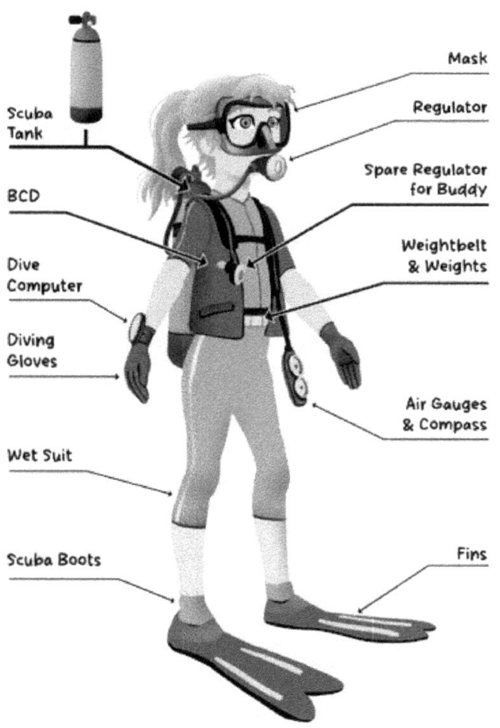

Photo Guide to Lucy's Underwater Animals

Chapter 1 - Brain Coral

Brain coral takes its name from the fact that it looks like a human brain. Brain coral is a community of thousands of tiny individual animals called coral polyps, living in a patterned structure made of calcium carbonate.

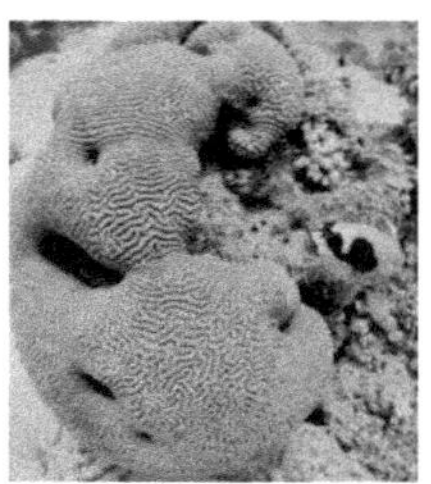

Chapter 1 - Staghorn Coral

Staghorn coral is made of thousands of little animals called coral polyps. Staghorn is a very prickly coral. It can scratch or cut your skin if you get too close. Small fish hide between the 'fingers' to escape predators.

Chapter 1 - Soft Corals

Soft corals form colonies of coral polyps, but they don't make a hard skeleton of calcium carbonate around their bodies. They take water inside themselves to act as a hydro-skeleton which holds them upright in the water so they can catch food. They can be found in many colours.

Chapter 1 - Sea Slugs

These are invertebrates, so have no backbone. Highly coloured and patterned, they have no eyes, just two horn-like structures on the top of their head which recognise light and dark. They extract oxygen from the water through the feathery structure on top of their bodies.

Chapter 1 - Turtles

Wonderful reptiles who are very friendly to divers. Need to surface to breathe oxygen from the atmosphere.

Chapter 1 - Purple Pipe Sponges

Sponges, in one form or another, have been on Earth for over 600 million years. They are tube-like animals which can grow up to 1.5 metres high. They remain sessile (not moving) and filter feed, like corals. They take hundreds of years to grow but are being damaged by oil spills and other pollution.

Chapter 1 - Crab

This photograph was taken in the Galapagos Islands in the Pacific Ocean. This crab is very colourful and scuttles around the rocks at the edge of the sea before entering the water to find food. Its eyes poke out at the top of its head.

Chapter 12 - Napoleon Wrasse

A very large fish, which is very friendly towards divers. It is often curious and swims up to say hello. Its lips move out from its mouth, forming a straw-like structure which it uses to suck up small fish for its meals.

Chapter 12 - Barracuda

A predatory fish with very sharp teeth. They grow to over one metre in length and often swim in shoals. These creatures can be very scary and divers tend to keep away from them. Keep your hands out of the way or your fingers could be their breakfast!

Chapter 13 - Arrowhead Crabs

A thin, spidery-looking crab which grows up to 20 cm. It has been found 165 metres below the surface in the darker parts of the oceans. It is nocturnal, and feeds on algae and small invertebrates.

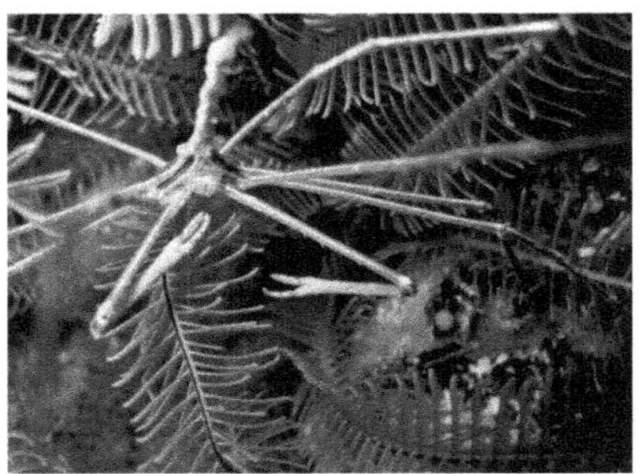

Chapter 13 - Sweetlips

These fish usually grow up to 60cm in length. Also known as grunts because these fish make strange noises by grinding their teeth. They hide in the coral during the day and hunt for small invertebrates at night.

Chapter 13 - Giant Clam

A clam is a mollusc related to snails, slugs and other shelled bi-valves (two-shelled animals which close for protection). The Giant Clam attaches itself to dead coral on reef tops and can grow up to 20 metres long. It filters sea water to extract food.

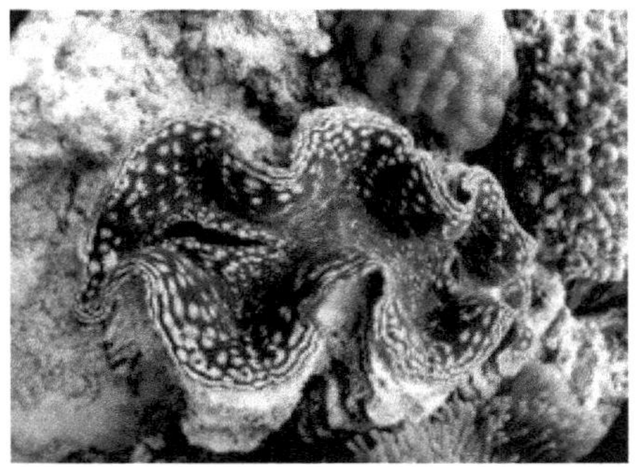

Chapter 13 - Stonefish

A stonefish has a bulbous-round body with amazing camouflage, a vertical mouth, tiny eyes and large pectoral fins (side fins). Found hiding in soft coral or on the sand it feeds on small fish and crustaceans (shrimp-like animals). It has poisonous spines along its back, which can be extremely painful - or even fatal! Grows to 38 cm.

Wiki Commons

Chapter 18 - Leaf-cutter ants

Leaf-cutter ants can carry up to 20 times their own body weight. Next to humans, leaf-cutter ants form the largest and most complex animal societies on Earth with their nests growing to more than 30m across and containing more than 8 million individuals.

Chapter 21 - Bat

Bats are mammals which can fly, and in the air they are more manoeuvrable than birds. Their finger bones are elongated and grow within the wings. They roost in caves and are nocturnal. Normally they eat insects or fruit but Vampire bats like blood! Not dangerous to humans but can carry diseases.

Chapter 21 - Swallow

These little birds are good at eating insects as they fly. They are long-distance migrants flying hundreds of miles to spend summers and winters in different parts of the world. They love nesting in caves, or old buildings.

Chapter 30 - Fusiliers

Always found in shoals, often containing hundreds of fish. Flashes of blue pass you by - and if you are in the way of the shoal - the fish merely swim around you as they move on through the water.

Chapter 36 - Blue Spotted Ray

Rays and sharks are related as they have a common ancestor, but rays look different as they have formed beautiful wing-like structures which help them move in the water. The blue-spotted ray is almost harmless, its sting is small.

Chapter 37 - Garden Eels

Garden eels are small fish which grow up to 40 cm long. They are shaped like an eel, with a tiny head, a large mouth and big eyes. They live in colonies of eels on sandy seabeds. Emerging from the sand and pointing in the direction of the current allows it to catch drifting food without leaving its burrow.

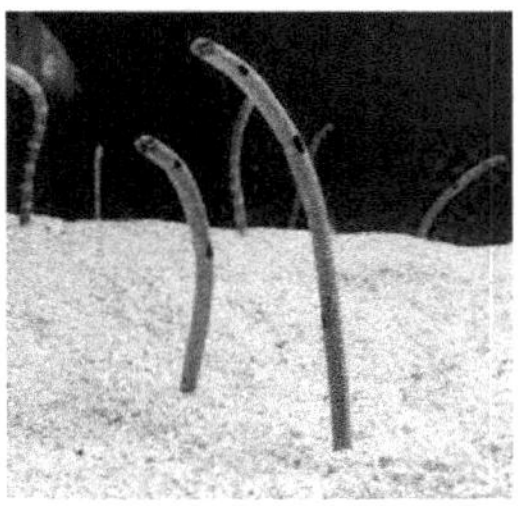

Chapter 37 - Goby & Shrimp

Goby fish sleep in burrows in the sandy seabed, but shrimps are better equipped to dig the hole. Some goby fish join with a species of blind shrimp as partners in protection from predators. The shrimp digs the hole and the goby watches out for predators. They both dash into the hole if a predator comes near.

Chapter 37 - Yellow-headed Jawfish

Jawfish are mouthbreeders, and it is the male of the species which carry the eggs of the young in their mouth until they hatch. These fish live in a burrow on the seabed, poking their heads above the sand to feed, but they are always on the lookout for predators and soon sink back into their burrows. Going up and down quickly, they look like tiny dancers.

Chapter 37 - Snake Eel

Snake eels can have tails up to 70 cm long. A snake eel slides its long tail into the sand, leaving only its head sticking out. It pops out to catch small fish swimming by but is well-hidden from predators when tucked up in the sand.

Chapter 37 - Peacock Flounder

Flounders are a species of fish found in shallow waters. When first born the fish is a 'normal' shape, but within a few weeks the fish has moved both eyes to one side of its body, rearranged its mouth and is almost completely flat, with an incredible camouflage pattern on its back, so it can't be seen on the seabed by predators.

Chapter 50 - Dolphins

Dolphins are mammals - not fish. They need to come to the surface to breathe air. They are very intelligent and love to play around the bows of a boat.

Chapter 50 - Manta Ray

The manta ray is the largest ray in the ocean. It can measure up to 7 metres across. Its large mouth is at the front of its body. It is a filter feeder and not a predator.

All photos © copyright to the author
unless otherwise stated.

Books by this Author
Children's Fiction - For children ages 8-13+
The Lucy Morgan Adventure Series

When Lucy leaves London for a new life in the Caribbean she becomes intrigued by life under the waves. These books not only deal with animals, nature and environment but also tells how children can 'make a difference'!

These Lucy Books have all been awarded Literary Titan 5 Star Gold Awards

Eye of the Turtle ISBN 9781838064303

The Secrets of the Shallows ISBN 9781838064327

The Hidden Cave ISBN 9781838064327

All books available from Amazon, all good book shops or direct from www.barnettauthor.co.uk

Non-Fiction - for ages 10 to 110

**The Amazing World Beneath the Waves
(A Guide to Understanding the Ocean)**

The information contained in this book includes life in the
oceans, the chemistry and physics of the oceans plus lots
more. With underwater photographs taken by divers from
around the world, this book s a gem for anyone wanting to
learn more about the oceans.

All the science is explained in everyday English - so it can
read by ages 10-110.

ISBN: 9781838064372

Teachers' Resources
for ages 8-12

Ocean World
Lesson FOUR

For Primary Schools, Secondary KS3, Science Clubs,
Home Learning and anywhere elsewhere children want to
learn.

Lots more Teacher Resources available at
www.gloria@barnettauthor.co.uk

About the Author

For over 30 years Gloria has been exploring our planet's oceans and has dived in a variety of areas around the world. She is a master scuba diver, keen sailor and underwater videographer as well as an educational advisor, science presenter and author.

Gloria works with schools in her guise as the 'Weird Fish Lady', presenting 'Underwater Adventure Days' and producing teachers' resources to inspire and encourage learning about the natural world.

Reviews

If you purchased your book through AMAZON, then you can also w
rite a review on their website – just go back to the AMAZON page where you purchased this book and add your review.
Your review gets published on the Amazon book page and could be read by millions of people around the world.

There is only one Planet Earth - it is our home - please look after it!

Footprint to the Future is a social enterprise producing teaching resources and books to help everyone understand Planet Earth.
Gloria is the lead science writer for this enterprise.

Acknowledgements

My family: Chris, my husband and special dive buddy, together with Matthew, Hannah and Becki's and my grandchildren, who all understood my need to share my knowledge and love of oceans. They supported me every step of the way.

Andrew who pushed, shoved and kicked me into writing fiction and then gave me enormous encouragement and insight as I honed my skills. Katrin for her early illustrations. Silva, Jane and Christine for reading early versions and not laughing too much when my stories seemed more like absurd manuals for learning to dive.

David for all his encouragement in the early stages.

Celia at Amber designs for sharing her amazing creativity, Rochelle for my website and Pauline for the proofreading The adults and children who have given their opinions as reviewers. More recently, Florian for his excellent cover illustrations.

... and last, but not least, Ryby and Tracy who patiently taught me how to dive and introduced me to the wonderful underwater world.

Thank you - everyone.